PUYALLUP

in

WORLD WAR II

PUYALLUP

in

WORLD WAR II

Hans Zeiger

THE
History
PRESS

Published by The History Press
Charleston, SC
www.historypress.com

Copyright © 2018 by Hans Zeiger
All rights reserved

First published 2018

Manufactured in the United States

ISBN 9781625859723

Library of Congress Control Number: 2018948032

Notice: The information in this book is true and complete to the best of our knowledge. It is offered without guarantee on the part of the author or The History Press. The author and The History Press disclaim all liability in connection with the use of this book.

Dedicated to Ruth and Andy Anderson.

CONTENTS

ACKNOWLEDGEMENTS

They died for a dream," Frank Failor, in a wheelchair in an assisted living facility in Seattle, told me one rainy day when we'd been talking for some time about the generation—his generation—that gave so much in the Second World War. "What was the dream?" I asked. The 1939 Puyallup High School graduate told me that it was the dream of a free society. The men and women of that generation embodied American ideals that were worth living for, even dying for. These men and women, from Puyallup and thousands of other communities, deserve our unending thanks.

Many of these good people made this book possible. This work is possible, most of all, because of several local people who lived through the war years and deliberately labored to document that time for the historical record. They include U.S. Army journalist Private First Class Mark Porter, Lieutenant Jackson Granholm, Major R. Vernon Hill, Major Stuart O. Van Slyke, longtime Puyallup Kiwanis Club historian W.R. Sandy and Tom Montgomery, who published the *Puyallup Valley Tribune* during the war. Others—including John Shirley, Howard Randall, Frank and Francisco Lovato, Romain Cansiere and Oscar Gilbert—provided written war accounts closely related to the experiences of Puyallup men overseas. A few other works—including Louis Fiset's *Camp Harmony*, Ron Magden's *Furusato*, James R. Warren's *The War Years: A Chronicle of Washington State in World War II* and the wonderful history of Puyallup by Lori Price and Ruth Anderson—also proved valuable.

Then there are the many people, connected to Puyallup directly or indirectly, who took time to talk with me. They are the veterans of the war, the men and women who carried on the war effort at home, the friends and family of men who were killed and Japanese Americans who lived through the war years. They spent time answering my interview questions on the phone, corresponding by mail and graciously hosting me in their living rooms or at their dining room tables. Members of the Puyallup High School classes of 1937 and 1939 invited me to reunion events, where I was able to learn so much about those graduates and their contributions to our country. I am grateful especially to the late Paul Harmes, a veteran of the South Pacific, who was retired from a long career running Puyallup Heating and Fuel. I went to visit him one evening late in 2007, and we ended up talking for about four hours. He gave me an impressive list of names and stories as well as a few phone numbers, and I started calling people to request interviews. It was from him that I first heard many of the names that fill these pages.

In this quest, I was blessed to spend time in the archives of the Puyallup Public Library, the Tacoma Public Library Northwest Room, the Puyallup Historical Society Collection at the Meeker Mansion, the Puyallup Kiwanis Club, Puyallup VFW Post 2224 and the Puyallup High School History Room. Special thanks to Ruth and Andy Anderson, Jan Baginski, Jeannie Knutson and Joan Kovacevich of the Puyallup Historical Society; Waunita and Dave Preston of the Puyallup High School History Room; Paul Herrera and Larry Heires of the VFW; Jan Baginski and Jeanie Veith of All Saints Catholic Parish; Julie Watts of the Fife Historical Society; Eileen Yamada Lamphere, Elsie Yotsuuye Taniguchi, Cho Shimizu and other members of the Puyallup Valley Japanese American Citizens League; Joshua Zimmerman of the Catholic Archdiocese of Seattle Archives; and Beth Swartzbaugh and the staff of the Puyallup Library.

I am indebted to a number of people who provided access to the private archive of a loved one, including Stan Barker, Mary Lutis Beaubien, Sara Martinson Carlington, Patty Carter, Kristin Hunt Cheney, Gene Humiston Cotton, Vernell Hill Doyle, Betty Porter Dunbar and Jerry Dunbar, Gloria Kelley Frederickson and Eric Garcia, Sparky Gamaunt, Jean Wilhelmsen Glaser, Bill Hanawalt, Barbara Jacobs, Barbara Martinson Jensen, Ruth Bigelow Jones, Terry Kandle, Chris Gilliam Nimick, Stanley Stemp, Dennis Ward, Gary Whitley and Lois and Cristi Williams.

Heather Meier, editor of the *Puyallup Herald*, was kind enough to give me space for articles once a month in 2008 and 2009. Much of this book began as articles for the *Herald*.

My wife, Erin, was patient as I spent hours in my study at work on the book, and she was exceedingly helpful as she gave feedback on chapter drafts. Andy Anderson, Ruth Anderson, Larry Bargmeyer, Reverend Nancy Gowler and Jack Taylor read the manuscript and provided excellent suggestions for improvements. I am grateful to History Press commissioning editor Artie Crisp and senior editor Ryan Finn for their terrific work.

There were disappointments in this work. Having finally come upon the phone number of some unsung battlefield hero or homefront champion, I would find that it was a disconnected number or learn that someone had recently passed on. And so, sadly, I didn't get all of the stories I wanted.

In any book like this, there will inevitably be stories left untold that truly should have been told. If I have overlooked anything or anyone, I hope someone will take the time to let me know so that I might add it to a collection of local stories I have only begun.

INTRODUCTION

More than a decade ago, while watching the interviews with World War II veterans that appear before the Tom Hanks and Steven Spielberg film series *Band of Brothers*, it occurred to me that the generation that fought that war was disappearing quickly. I thought of the veterans I knew back home in Puyallup, some of whom I had met in high school when I was involved with the dedication of the Veterans Memorial statue in Pioneer Park. Who were the dozens of men from Puyallup whose names were engraved on the pedestal of the statue because they had died during the war?

What were they like when they were growing up in the same place where I grew up? What was the town like then? And how is it that an entire generation from our community and from every community in the country could have served in such extraordinary ways?

As I thought about my little corner of the country during a big war, it occurred to me that I needed to learn some old stories—if only I could find the right people to share them. After watching Ken Burns's great documentary *The War*, a study of World War II through the experiences of four American towns, I was inspired about the possibility of immersing myself in my own town to learn its wartime stories. I decided that I would learn everything I could about Puyallup during World War II.

This book is the result of my search. There are lessons in these stories for all of the generations that have succeeded the "Greatest Generation," as Tom Brokaw called them. Through their stories, words and memories, I hope that I can help to make those lessons meaningful.

Chapter 1

THE GENEROUS PEOPLE

In 1937, a Swedish American carpenter named Nicholas Hogman of Sangamon County, Illinois, sold almost everything he owned, purchased a truck and built benches in its bed and a canopy over the top. His wife, Mary, sat in the back in a rocking chair, surrounded by seven of their children, as two more sat in the cab with Nicholas. Their eighteen-year-old son, who had never driven a truck before, took the wheel all the way to Issaquah, Washington. The price tag on the weeklong road trip, truck included, was seventy-five dollars.

Relatives in Issaquah advised the Hogmans to seek work in the berry fields of Puyallup. So, the family spent the summer of 1937 picking berries. Soon Nicholas found work on a cherry farm in Sumner and bought a little house on Twenty-Third Avenue Northeast. Somehow they made ends meet. "We could make fifty dollars a season picking berries," recalled Manford Hogman. "And that would buy us all of our school clothes and supplies and everything we needed."[1]

The Hogmans understood the word *need*. So did the Stemp family. In all of 1935, Stanley Stemp made eighty dollars from his Riverside berry, rabbit and chicken farm. With his daughter graduating from Puyallup High School in June, Stanley stretched his money to ensure that she could celebrate in style. "We had a dress-up day on the last day of school," Eleanore recalled. "The girls got dressed up in new outfits. Mamma took me into Tacoma to get a suit. She didn't have enough money for shoes, so she had to borrow five dollars from my sister."

Young Barbara Martinson on the sidewalk outside of her parents' store, Queen City Grocery, along Meridian Street in the early 1930s. *Courtesy of Sara Martinson Carlington.*

Not everyone in the class of 1935 was so fortunate. Eleanore's cousin was among those who couldn't pull together the funds for dress-up day. She stayed home. "Those are the kinds of things that hurt your feelings when you couldn't do the things that others did," said Eleanore.[2]

Eleanore's cousin Stanley said, "We didn't get to play much." He managed to play basketball at school as long as he was back on the farm doing chores

A group of boys from J.P. Stewart Elementary School after winning the school basketball tournament, early 1930s. Frank Hanawalt holds the ball. *Courtesy of Bill Hanawalt.*

right afterward. "We came home and had duties to do: clean the pig pens every Saturday, every night clean the cow and horse stalls; when you're done with the chicken stalls, pick up the eggs. Every night you had to chop old cedar berry poles for kindling. If in the middle of the night dad didn't find it there, he'd wake you up to go get it. It was hard to learn, but that's how you learned."[3]

In the Depression days, people felt a sense of responsibility, the realization that a mother and father, a grandparent or a grandchild, a daughter and son, depended on you. It shaped the character of a generation. Describing his high school classmates, Hogman recalled, "If they had anything, they had to work for it. The kids all had to work. Everybody who had more than a city lot had raspberries and blackberries growing on it."[4]

But according to Eleanore, "There were a lot of advantages about that era—not as many things to amuse themselves with, but they learned how to work."[5] They also learned how to give. When the occasional hungry Tacoman wandered down River Road and showed up on their back porch, the Stemps always had chicken from the farm to give away.[6]

For all the impoverishments of the age, the people of Puyallup were rich in a way. Amid work, people found time to celebrate the passages of life. The Daffodil Festival began in 1933. The berries followed the daffodils, and Puyallup was proud to host the Western Washington Fair in September. Even if rain watered the rich soil and muddied Viking Field before the rivalry with Sumner, people turned out to cheer on the Puyallup High School Vikings football team.

For people who called Puyallup home, the town offered a sense of place to those who were born there or moved there, on the condition that they could give back something to their neighbors when they were able.

FROM PUYALLUP TO BERLIN

In the course of the 1930s, people in Puyallup had a growing awareness of certain events and personalities in far-off places. Dean Vernon McKenzie of the University of Washington visited the Puyallup Kiwanis Club on June 29, 1933, and talked about a new leader in Germany named Adolf Hitler. A professor from the College of Puget Sound visited the Kiwanis Club the following year and discussed the "Crisis in Germany," as the records of the Kiwanis Club of Puyallup show.

In 1936, Puyallup sent two of its own off to the Olympic Games in Berlin. One was Gertrude Stelling Wilhelmsen, a javelin and discus thrower and one of the few American athletes of the 1936 games who was fluent in German. Her mother died in the 1919 flu epidemic. She and her siblings were raised by their German-speaking father on a Puyallup farm. A member of the Puyallup High School track-and-field team, she set a world record in the javelin throw as a senior in 1931.[7]

Wilhelmsen got her start in track and field at Puyallup High School in the late 1920s. At the age of twenty-three, married to Andrew Wilhelmsen and the mother of two children, she qualified for the Olympics in javelin and discus. Puyallup High School track and field coach Robert "Pop" Logan was convinced that Wilhelmsen could achieve greatness in the javelin throw. He invited her to practice with the PHS men's track-and-field team after she graduated in 1931, and he encouraged her to try out for the 1932 Olympic Games. She nearly qualified. She was determined to make the cut in 1936.[8]

Wilhelmsen, along with her sister, Hildegard Stelling Sierman, made arrangements to take part in the Olympic trials at Providence, Rhode Island. Sierman vied to compete in the eighty-meter and one-hundred-meter hurdles. To pay for Wilhelmsen, Sierman and Logan to travel to the East Coast, Fred Flannigan chaired a fundraising committee for the Puyallup Young Men's Business Club, and several members of the club went throughout the city soliciting funds.[9] In the days leading up to the

Theo Last Star of the Blackfeet Nation helps Gertrude Stelling Wilhelmsen to prepare for the 1936 Olympic trials. *Courtesy of Jean Wilhelmsen Glaser.*

trip east, Wilhelmsen practiced her field events at Viking Field. In shot put practice, she set a new women's world record of 40 feet, 8 inches, besting the previous record by 20 inches. And two days before leaving for Providence, on July 1, Wilhelmsen set a women's world record in the discus throw: 136 feet, 8 inches.[10]

Wilhelmsen succeeded in the Olympic trials (although her sister did not), but she faced one more obstacle: paying for her trip to Germany in the middle of the Depression. Short on funds for its teams, the U.S. Olympic Committee asked community partners across the country to pitch in. From Providence, Coach Logan went into action and did everything he could to appeal to Puyallup's business and civic leaders, as well as local press. He needed to raise $500. "It would be a pitiful shame, if this young woman could not make the trip she earned," he wrote. "But there isn't much time. Expense money must be in by the 15th."[11] By the time the quote was published in the *Tacoma Times*, less than a week remained until the deadline.

Once again, the Puyallup Young Men's Business Club took a lead role, deciding that "the success of a young woman, a product of Puyallup, was as important as the success of any of our commercial products," Coach Logan wrote for a local paper, adding, "I think this demonstrates the cooperative spirit of our town….Puyallup will never regret backing her up morally or financially."[12] Other communities around the country rallied for their hometown athletes in similar ways.[13] Funds came together quickly, and on July 12, three days before the deadline, Logan was able to send the following telegram to Wilhelmsen in New York from his travel stop in Duluth, Minnesota: "Am happy to learn enough money came in to take entire team to Berlin Can return home feeling trip not wasted…. Congratulations to all you girls…for your splendid fight Bonvoyage and success Write me from Berlin."[14]

And so Wilhelmsen was off to Berlin on the Olympic team ship SS *President Roosevelt.* "The best wishes of your hometown folk follow you on to Berlin," the Young Men's Business Club wired to Wilhelmsen in Providence.[15] "Bon voyage, Gertrude and George, and good luck," noted an editorial in the *Puyallup Valley Tribune.*[16]

Track and field star Gertrude Stelling Wilhelmsen on board the SS *President Roosevelt* from New York to Germany for the 1936 Olympic Games. *Courtesy of Jean Wilhelmsen Glaser.*

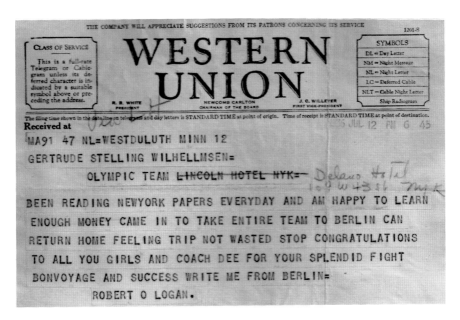

Telegram from Puyallup High School coach Robert "Pop" Logan to Wilhelmsen after funds came in for her to go to the 1936 Olympic Games. *Jean Wilhelmsen Glaser Collection.*

Wilhelmsen training on board the SS *President Roosevelt*. *Jean Wilhelmsen Glaser Collection.*

Gertrude Wilhelmsen and fellow athletes after arriving in Berlin. *Jean Wilhelmsen Glaser Collection.*

Wilhelmsen was the only American track-and-field competitor who spoke German, which came in handy as she and fellow Olympic athletes made their way around Berlin. She attended a dinner with German propaganda minister Joseph Goebbels and Hermann Goering, but she declined an invitation to meet Adolf Hitler in order to watch her teammate Jesse Owens run one of his sprints. After the Olympics, she would join Owens as his shuffleboard competitor on the ship back to New York.[17] Wilhelmsen was in proximity with Hitler on more than one occasion during the games. "I could have touched him on the shoulder," she said.[18]

Right: Members of the women's U.S. Olympic track team and two men, including an Italian athlete. Gertrude Stelling Wilhelmsen is second from left. *Courtesy of Jean Wilhelmsen Glaser.*

Below: Puyallup athlete Gertrude Stelling Wilhelmsen looks on as an Olympic teammate signs a visitor log in Wuppertal, Germany, following the 1936 Berlin Olympic Games. *Courtesy of Jean Wilhelmsen Glaser.*

Placing seventh in the discus and ninth in the javelin competitions, Wilhelmsen stood out as the top American in both of her sports.[19] Although shot put was not an Olympic event, Wilhelmsen went on to compete in the shot put in a separate competition in Wupertal. She placed fourth in the contest.[20]

SHORTY

The other 1936 Olympic athlete from Puyallup was George Hunt, a member of the University of Washington's rowing team. Standing six feet, three inches but widely known as "Shorty," Hunt had been a popular student athlete at Puyallup High School, playing football, basketball and tennis; serving as class treasurer; and excelling in academics. He graduated at the age of sixteen in 1933 and went on to the university, where he joined the rowing team, as Daniel James Brown noted in his 2013 work, *The Boys in the Boat: Nine Americans and Their Epic Quest for Gold at the 1936 Berlin Olympics.*

The crew of nine that became the United States Olympic rowing team first gained fame in 1934 when, as freshmen, they rowed to a surprise victory in the famous Poughkeepsie Regatta.[21] Husky crew coach Al Ulbrickson took his time assembling a boat that he believed could qualify for and win in the Olympics, and Shorty made the cut.

Hunt was hardworking, gregarious and opinionated, and he could become especially nervous at times. As a crew member, he had a gift for encouraging his fellow rowers.[22]

At the Olympic trials in Princeton, New Jersey, the University of Washington crew came together and delivered a stunning victory. The unified strokes that brought the shell home on the final stretch were "the best I ever felt in any boat," Hunt wrote home to his parents in Puyallup the day after the race.[23] And now they were bound for Berlin. "A dream come true! Oh boy, what lucky kids we are! Nobody can tell me we didn't have Old Dame Luck perched on our shoulders," he wrote.[24]

At Hamburg, on the way to Berlin, the U.S. Olympic crew team "just sat and took it" as the Bürgermeister delivered a lengthy speech that they couldn't understand, he wrote.[25] When their train arrived at the Berlin station, they were greeted by thousands of Germans. "It made you feel very much like a freak in a sideshow—pointing at you with their mouths open and saying something about zwei meter, meaning of course, that we were two meters tall—over six feet," Hunt wrote home.[26]

The opening of the Olympic Games happened to fall on Shorty Hunt's twentieth birthday. "Maybe that's another lucky sign," he wrote.[27] The crew team endured the ostentatious Nazi opening ceremonies, where Hunt was struck by the dramatic marching of the German soldiers and the entry of Adolf Hitler.[28]

· · · · · · · · · · · · · · · · ·

SHORTY HUNT WRITES HOME FROM NAZI GERMANY
Letter to Mr. and Mrs. Elwood Hunt, Puyallup Valley Tribune, *August 21, 1936, 1.*

August 5, 1936
Grunau

Dear Folks,
...The formal opening of the games...fell on my birthday. We had a turnout in the morning but none in the afternoon because of the ceremonies. A special train started at Kopenich at 1 o'clock with all the rowers and canoers aboard. We had to go pretty slow because of the great crowds of people. It took about an hour to get to the stadium. About an hour was taken up in telling us some of the preliminaries—such as where we were to line up, how to salute, when to salute and where to line up after we were in the stadium—when and if we got there!
*   With some time to kill, some of us wandered out through a gateway beneath the Bell Tower, and arrived just in time to see some of Hitler's crack troops going through their paces. There were three batteries: one of the regular army, the marines and the aviators. They were all within an inch of one another's height and so far as training and discipline—I don't think they could be [equaled] any place in the world. They were marching around when at a certain signal, they all started goose-stepping. You couldn't hear yourself think for all the noise they were making. They had the whole bottom of their shoes covered with hob nails, and they were throwing their feet down so hard the dust was flying off the granite rock they were marching on. Even the horses were goose-stepping*

*and doing it at the command of the officers. For precision and
timing they could not be beaten.*

*We then had to line up and after doing so, the big Olympic
Bell was rung to signify the arrival of Hitler. The teams of
the different nations were lined up on either side of the polo
field and Hitler marched down through the middle saluting
each country in turn—Germany first, United States second,
Uruguay third, and so [forth] up the alphabet.*

*After Hitler had taken his seat of honor, the nations
commenced marching in. Going off to one side of the stadium,
they marched down through a tunnel and came into the
stadium itself—marched around the track in front of Hitler
and then took their places on the field again in alphabetical
order. Quite a ceremony took place, but all in German, so we
could not understand a word they said. It all ended up with
Hitler opening the games formally in a few words—and a
very husky voice.*

．．．．．．．．．．．．．．．．．

When it came time for the race on the Langer See, it was a slow start
for the American team. They fought strong winds and found it difficult to
communicate amid the roar of the vast crowds.[29] But in the final moments
of the race, as Adolf Hitler watched from his platform, Shorty Hunt of
Puyallup and his eight crewmates passed the German and Italian teams and
won gold.[30] Hunt, *Seattle Post Intelligencer* sports writer Royal Brougham said,
was, along with Coach Ulbrickson in his own rowing days, one of the two
greatest crew members in University of Washington history.[31]

Shorty Hunt and Gertrude arrived home to a hero's welcome in September.
Their friends in Puyallup held a grand ceremony for them at the Puyallup Fair.[32]
Wilhelmsen told a local newspaper, "I wish you'd tell the Puyallup people for me
how very much I appreciate the help they gave me to make the trip....I certainly
appreciate what Puyallup did."[33]

NAVY ENSIGN SHORTY HUNT

George "Shorty" Hunt joined the Navy Construction Battalion in 1942, and he trained in Norfolk, Virginia, for a few weeks. He was commissioned an ensign the following year. He had gone to the South Pacific with the Seabees by early 1943. Remembering the moment in 1936 when he was crowned by Hitler, he wrote home, "I certainly would like the chance to crown Hitler." Then there came a time when Hunt was a guest in the canoe of a native islander in the Admiralty Islands. He wrote home to his mother in the summer of 1944 describing the canoe journey. This must have been a time of wonder to the former member of the University of Washington rowing team and co-victor of the 1936 Berlin Olympics.

Puyallup Valley Tribune, "Hunt Becomes Naval Officer," November 6, 1942, 1; *Puyallup Press,* "Would Like to Crown Hitler," January 21, 1944; August 18, 1944.

" THE WORLD IS IN CHAOS"

After graduating from Puyallup High School in 1935, Stuart Van Slyke went to the University of Washington and took part in the Army Reserve Officer Training Corps. To him, it was obvious that a war was about to begin. "[I]f you had read 'Mein Kampf,' written by Adolf Hitler who started what Germany planned to do, if you read the daily paper, Germany was rearming and even an idiot could see that in the very near future, 'All Hell Was Going to Break Loose.'"[34]

"The world is in chaos," Van Slyke's mother, Amy Dobson Van Slyke, wrote in her diary on September 26, 1938, the day Stuart left Puyallup to begin his junior year at the University of Washington. "Hitler today said he was going to occupy the Sudetan area October 1st. It seems as though nothing will stop him. France, England and Russia are pledged to help Czecho-Slovakia."[35]

In Puyallup four years after the Berlin Olympics, war seemed to some like a real possibility, although the topic was debatable. War was raging in Europe, but it still seemed so distant. "Isolationist Pacifism vs. Economic Participation of the U.S. in the Present World Conflict" was the topic of a debate by the College of Puget Sound debate team before the Puyallup Kiwanis Club on May 23, 1940.[36] For the annual joint picnic of the Kiwanis Club and the Women's Chamber of Commerce at Grayland Park on August 1, a traveler named George Hellyer addressed more than five hundred attendees on "How to Defend America; If England Falls, then We Are Next."[37]

With Congressional approval of a draft that September, men began to register for the draft on October 16. More than 920 men registered in

15th Infantry, 3rd Squadron, 2nd Platoon, H Company, training at Fort Lewis, 1941. Corporal Stafford T. Carter (*standing at far right*) settled in Puyallup after the war. *Courtesy of Patty Carter.*

the Puyallup draft. Other kinds of employment opportunities arose in the region, including major federal contracts with the Boeing Company that brought 7,500 job openings that fall. A new National Guard anti-tank unit—Company A of the 103rd Anti-Tank Battalion—was formed from 35 initial volunteers in Puyallup and Sumner under the command of Lieutenant Phil Dickey of Puyallup, and 21 men began training in February 1941.[38]

Lieutenant Doug Kelley in the Battle of Britain

It came as no surprise to people in Puyallup when Doug Kelley joined the Royal Canadian Air Force in 1939. Kelley took up flying in his teen years, saving his money from a job delivering telegrams and special mail to pay for lessons and plane rentals.[39] Taking off from the little airstrip along the river, he would come down low over his girlfriend's house in the Riverside area, buzzing in for a noisy greeting. "He did things our parents shuddered at," his classmate Frank Hanawalt recalled. "We all thought it was great."[40]

"He was always pulling something," said his friend Earl White. "He was a pretty darn nice guy on top of it."[41]

It wasn't long after graduation from Puyallup High School in 1939 that Doug joined the Royal Canadian Air Force. Although America would not be at war for another two and a half years, Doug's ambitions for glory transcended the national border. With training, Kelley was off to England for the Battle of Britain. He commanded a night-fighter in the Nazi-laden sky over London in the fateful summer of 1940.

"Knowing what a tough cookie and a wild man Kelley was, I felt sorry for the German air-crews," wrote Jackson Granholm, Kelley's high school chemistry lab partner and later a navigator on bombing raids over Germany with the 8th Army Air Force.[42]

After graduating from Puyallup High School in 1939, Doug Kelley joined the Royal Canadian Air Force and flew in the Battle of Britain. Courtesy of Gloria Kelley Fredrickson.

Although outnumbered by the Germans, Kelley and his fellow pilots from Britain and allied nations won the battle and saved Great Britain; 544 of the nearly 3,000 allied flyers in the Battle of Britain were killed. "Never, in the field of human conflict was so much owed by so many to so few," said British prime minister Winston Churchill.[43] Kelley was among the surviving "few."

After the United States entered the war, Lieutenant Doug Kelley returned home from his service with the Royal Canadian Air Force and went to work for Uncle Sam. The U.S. Army Air Corps assigned him to lead advanced air training at an air base in Florida. After months of teaching his craft to the rising generation of flyers, Kelley was apparently restless. He wanted to get back into the action of war. His request for transfer to the South Pacific was granted.

In October 1943, Doug came home to Puyallup on furlough. His brother, Jack, a field artilleryman then stationed at Fort Ord, was also home. For the two brothers; their sister, Gloria; and their mother, Florence, it was the first time their little family had been together for three years.[44]

In December, Lieutenant Kelley flew over the Pacific in a P-38 or a P-70 to join up with the 419th Night Fighter Squadron under the 13th Air Force newly arrived at Guadalcanal. The 419th went to Guadalcanal to reinforce the 6th Night Fighter Squadron, Detachment B, which had been flying P-38 and P-70 patrols in the area since February. The P-70s flew best under ten thousand feet, only half the altitude of the Japanese bombers. When the superior P-38s were brought to Guadalcanal, the difficulty of spotting enemy planes in the dark of night from an altitude of thirty thousand feet made it nearly impossible to intercept the Japanese until ground crews turned searchlights onto the offending bombers.[45]

Lieutenant Kelley and the 419th had a difficult and dangerous project ahead of them. On his night mission

Lieutenant Doug Kelley after he returned to the United States to join his own country's war effort. *Courtesy of Gloria Kelley Fredrickson.*

Lieutenant Doug
Kelley home with
family in Puyallup.
*Courtesy of Gloria
Kelley Fredrickson.*

of January 10, 1944, Lieutenant Kelley's plane went down in the Pacific. He was reported as MIA. Florence Kelley learned that her son was missing a few weeks later.

"He wanted to live life to the fullest," said his sister Gloria. "If he couldn't have flown, he wouldn't have been happy. He told mom, 'If something happens when I'm flying, don't feel bad.' That's what brought us all through."[46]

WHICH WAY AMERICA?

Home in Puyallup from five years working for the Standard Vacuum Oil Company in China, where he had survived repeated Japanese attacks on Chinese cities, Vernon Hill spent most of 1941 warning anyone in Puyallup and surrounding areas who would listen to him that war with Japan was imminent. He described the horrors he had seen in China and urged people to think beyond Europe to the threat in the Pacific. He showed videos he had made and presented a map of the Pacific indicating where the Japanese might attack, including the Philippines, Guam and Hawaii. He spoke to church groups, service clubs, fraternal groups, a women's group, Mr. Ray Warren's history class at Puyallup High School and in private homes.[47] There were skeptics in these audiences. Ruth Riser of the Puyallup Junior Women's Club wrote an account of a presentation he made to her club: "One of the husbands, a high school history teacher, had a decided difference of opinion

A horse sale for U.S. Army purchasers was held at the Puyallup Fairgrounds on October 20, 1940. About one hundred people attended, many of them local farmers. Of thirty-five horses inspected, only two met U.S. Army physical specifications. *Tacoma Public Library, Richards Studio Collection, D120372.*

on the possibility of war with Japan claiming that Japan would not attack us. Vernon replied that Japan was preparing for such a conflict, and said we would be at war with Japan within a year, a year and a half at the latest."[48]

The 1941 Puyallup High School commencement ceremonies included four class panelists addressing the question of "Which Way America?" Leah Kennedy, Wayne Snider, valedictorian Sue Hendrickson and student body president Harold Jacobsen articulated the different perspectives: "All Out Aid to Britain," "Isolation," "Internationalism" and "Negotiated Peace."[49] This same, often heated debate was being repeated in cities and towns all across the country.

People from all over the Northwest went to the Puyallup Fair, as usual, in September 1941. They enjoyed the sights and sounds and tastes, the animals and the Valley produce, the rides and the games. No one in Puyallup could know then the full impact that war would have on them or the community.

Chapter 2

PEARL HARBOR

As Japanese planes tipped with the Rising Sun emblem struck hard out of a Sunday dawn, some thirty Puyallup mothers, wives and sweethearts realized their loved ones were trapped in a war that stunned and horrified America's millions.
—Puyallup Valley Tribune,
"Puyallup Men Fight Japanese in Pacific War," December 12, 1941

Late on December 6, 1941, a dozen B-17 "Flying Fortresses" left Hamilton Field, California, bound for the Philippines. In the copilot's seat on plane no. 7 of the 38th Reconnaissance Squadron sat Lieutenant Leonard Smith Humiston of Puyallup.

Len joined the U.S. Army Air Corps immediately after graduating from Puyallup High School in 1935, training to fill the posts of mechanic, gunner and pilot. Earlier in 1941, he married a nurse from Puyallup named Frances Nelson in a ceremony at Pioneer Baptist Church, across the street from the Meeker Mansion.[1]

Now on the blue sky Pacific morning of Sunday, December 7, the radio of Lieutenant Humiston's B-17 was playing Hawaiian tunes on radio station KGMB. The planes were scheduled to stop for refueling at Hickam Air Base, Hawaii.

In Pearl Harbor ahead, Lieutenant Humiston could make out smoke. He said he guessed that the navy was welcoming the incoming Flying Fortresses with a twenty-one-gun salute. When a swarm of fighter planes sped toward them, they expected a friendly escort to Hickam.

1940

Right: Lieutenant Leonard Smith Humiston. *Courtesy of Gene Humiston Cotton.*

Below: Lieutenant Leonard Humiston and his airplane. *Courtesy of Gene Humiston Cotton.*

L.S. HUMISTON

Len about "40"

Then reality hit. Those fighter planes were not American planes, and that smoke in Pearl Harbor was something other than a navy welcome. As Humiston's pilot, Lieutenant Robert Richards, prepared to land at Hickam, a Japanese Mitsubishi A6M2, known as the "Zero," buzzed around the B-17 and began pounding it with machine gun fire. There was little that the unarmed American plane could do except abort the landing and fly east, back out over the ocean.

At sea, Richards steered the plane back to Hawaii, this time for a downwind landing at Bellows Field. The Flying Fortress bounced onto the runway at high speed, and Richards could not slow it down in time. The B-17 crossed the end of the runway and skidded into a ditch. But the troubles weren't over on this completely unexpected combat morning. Japanese Zeroes spotted the downed plane in the ditch. One after another, the Zeroes strafed the helpless B-17, riddling it with bullets. Two of the B-17 crew members were wounded, but Humiston was uninjured.

When they finally got out to look for refuge at Bellows, Lieutenant Humiston and his crew had survived the first American air combat of World War II. Others in the group from Hamilton Field were not so lucky.[2]

Other Puyallup men were at Pearl Harbor that day. They included Ensign Verne Jennings, a former Puyallup High School music supervisor who had been called up for service in the navy reserve. Puyallup High School graduate Earl Dalton was assigned to a destroyer at Pearl Harbor. Radioman First Class Harold Brown was on board the USS *Nevada*, one year into his navy service. *Nevada* was badly damaged by Japanese bombs. Seaman First Class Harold Hukill of South Hill was uninjured when the USS *Helena* was hit. Seaman Second Class Vernon Brouillet, a crew member of the USS *New Orleans*, also came through the battle, as did Pharmacist Mate First Class Edmund Baldwin, who was stationed at Naval Hospital Pearl Harbor.[3]

Sunday Morning in Puyallup

Back home, the midday sun was shining through Ralph Smith's window on Sixth Street Southwest as he looked after his eleven-month-old son, who was born on New Year's Day 1941. Outside, his wife worked in the yard. After graduating from Puyallup High School in 1936, Ralph had served in the navy aboard the USS *Louisville* for three years, and now he had a job at Boeing and a little family. As he looked over his blessings, the radio buzzed in the background. An announcer's voice interrupted Ralph's concentration. It was a news bulletin. Pearl Harbor had been attacked.

Ralph wasn't entirely surprised. "We knew we were going to fight the Japanese, we always knew that. It was just such a tense feeling about that."[4]

Five blocks down Sixth Street from the Smiths, Betty Porter was home for the weekend with a friend from the University of Washington band, about to get on the road back to Seattle for a performance. When Betty was informed of the attack, she could not have known the price that her family would pay in the years to come.[5]

Many Puyallup residents learned of Pearl Harbor as late morning church services let out. Len Humiston's family heard the news as they left First Christian Church. "He might be over there," his sister Gene worried.[6]

Bernice Cook was singing in the choir at Christ Episcopal Church that morning:

> *We had just finished the service on that December Sunday morning and were preparing to take off our choir robes when one of our members who had stayed home that morning burst into the choir room to announce, "Pearl Harbor has been bombed!" Standing there stunned, we overheard four strangers—two of them men in uniform—asking Dr. [Archie] Sidders if he would marry one of the couples. When he agreed, we decided that we would also wish the young couple Godspeed by witnessing the ceremony and thereupon filed back into the choir stalls. Whether we sang something, I don't remember, but we added our blessings to the minister's.[7]*

At Seattle Pacific College, rumors of Pearl Harbor spread through the dormitory hall where former Puyallup High School student body president Marie Jones lived. She joined a little assembly down the hall. "One of the girls was from Hawaii, and I'll never forget that," said Jones. "It was very hard on her. We gathered around and listened to the radio, and cried, mostly."[8]

Jim Riley of Puyallup was also in Seattle, working at the Boeing factory. Riley had gone on lunch break. A few workers learned of Pearl Harbor on their radios. A din of voices began to crescendo through the building. "You could hear the volume of people who'd heard on the radio," said Riley.[9]

Among Japanese Americans who lived in the Puyallup Valley, news of the attack was especially shocking. Nineteen-year-old Bob Mizukami of Fife was competing in his second game at the annual Tacoma Furuya Alley Cats bowling tournament at the Broadway Bowling Alley when the radio was turned up with the bulletin about Pearl Harbor. Tom Takemura of Puyallup was at home listening to the noon news when he heard about the attacks. Through the window, Takemura saw women running in the fields to where their husbands, sons and brothers were laboring. Takemura picked up the phone to spread the word, but the lines were jammed.[10]

"I remember I ran home around 1:00," recalled John Watanabe of Firwood. "I knew Gene Autry was going to be on the radio. They kept breaking in and telling military personnel to report to camp. I said, 'What the hell is going on?'"[11]

For the Fort Lewis soldiers at Mount Rainier on December 7 training for ski patrols, the news had immediate implications. Don Henderson of Puyallup was skiing on the mountain when the soldiers arrived. First he noticed that they were wearing white capes. Then he noticed that they were making an abrupt retreat, heading out the way they'd come not long before. "All of the sudden, they were leaving, getting off the mountain. I skied down to the bottom and said to this guy, 'You guys just got there. Why are you leaving?'"

"Haven't you heard?" came the reply. "Pearl Harbor was just bombed."

So it was that Henderson, too, joined the day's traffic off the mountain, off and away to a world at war. Henderson joined the navy and was stationed for nearly a year and a half at Pearl Harbor. It would be among his tasks to recover corpses from the sunken USS *Oklahoma* in January 1943.

"When they raised the Oklahoma, they sent me over there, and a guy threw a gray thing at me," he recalled. "It was a muck suit. I put it on. They were pumping the compartments out. When they righted the thing, they'd pump it out and we'd get the bodies out....You'd grab a guy and the arm would come off....All we could smell was oil. Everything was full of oil. That's really the reason you wore a mucksuit. A lot of times you'd bring them out in pieces, put them in big old gray bodybags."[12]

The USS *Nevada* fared better than the *Oklahoma* on December 7. Radioman First Class Harold Brown survived, as did his ship.[13] After temporary repairs, *Nevada* ambled across the Pacific to the Bremerton Naval Shipyard. There Al Gerstmann of Puyallup went to work on the repairs.

When the guns of the *Nevada* pounded off the coast of Normandy during the Allied invasion of France a few years later, Gerstmann was there to hear them. From the English Channel, they volleyed inland past Omaha Beach to where the Germans were encamped. "My ears are still ringing from that concussion," he said.[14]

But on Monday, December 8, Gerstmann's ears were tuned to the voice of President Roosevelt as he addressed the nation at war. The radio echoed through the Puyallup High School commons, where hundreds of students were gathered. "It was very quiet and solemn," said Jane Bader Trimbley, a junior at the time. "I don't think any of us realized how dire it was and how big the sacrifice would be." Jane's boyfriend, Gordon Barker, joined the army right after graduation. He would be killed in the Battle of the Bulge.[15]

WARTIME IN PUYALLUP

And so Puyallup, and all the rest of the country, was at war. "It was war time and Puyallup took it big," stated the *Puyallup Valley Tribune*.[16] People packed into the Odd Fellows Hall that Monday evening to learn about what they could do to protect their homes and community. American Legion commander Lester Robinson chaired the meeting, and speakers included Mac Stevenson, chair of the Legion's Disaster and Relief Committee, along with Stella Ellison, chair of the Emergency Voluntary Service Committee; Puyallup police chief Jack Lenfesty; Puyallup fire chief Chester Brakefield; and local defense commissioner Tom Montgomery. "A large number of volunteers will be needed for civilian defense to assist as voluntary firemen and police, in first aid, and in many other branches of the services," said Montgomery, Puyallup's state representative as well as publisher of the *Puyallup Valley Tribune*.[17]

Before audiences like the one gathered at the Odd Fellows Hall that night, through his newspaper and through word of mouth, Montgomery instructed Puyallup residents to be on the ready for air raids, monitoring their radios and blacking out their windows. Every house and every business was required to have a water bucket, a sand bucket and a shovel or rake at the ready to put out incendiary bombs.[18]

Montgomery headed a Home Defense Auxiliary Unit with male and female participants. Women volunteered as administrators and ambulance drivers, while men took infantry roles.[19]

Local Boy Scouts official Jim Brown was named as Puyallup's chief air raid warden. The city was split into three air raid zones, each with a zone warden (LeRoy DeBolt, Lester Robertson and Clyde Gregory were Puyallup's three wardens) and three precincts led by precinct wardens; 417 block wardens were appointed throughout the city.[20]

A tower on top of the six-story Hunt Brothers cannery building along the railroad tracks, Puyallup's tallest building, was designated as the city's air raid watch tower. Twenty-four-hour operations began shortly after America's entry into the war, with H.E. Barney and Floyd Chase serving as chief observers. Local civic and fraternal groups helped to recruit volunteers. Women stood watch for twelve-hour shifts during the day, and men were on duty at night. Volunteers were charged with reporting any aircraft within sight; a phone was installed with a direct link to the inceptor command in Seattle. Altogether, more than one hundred Puyallup residents volunteered for air raid watch duty.[21]

Boy Scouts volunteered as fire watchers under the supervision of air raid wardens to aid with putting out bombs and fires in the event of an attack.[22] Local emergency managers and air raid officials coordinated a mock raid in February 1942. Following the sounding of an air raid siren from the fire station, they simulated property damage, a fire and injuries to test the responses of home defense auxiliary members, as well as local homeowners.[23]

Tynni Holm Martinson was among the many women who volunteered their mornings at the air raid watch tower atop the cannery building in downtown Puyallup. *Courtesy of Sara Martinson Carlington.*

A new observation tower on the top of the Puyallup City Hall opened in August 1942, replacing the cannery tower. Women took key roles in the new control room: Margaret Utzinger was the chief plotting officer, Pearl Hill was the record clerk and Mrs. John Bunns, Mrs. Jack Reynolds and Mrs. Charles Delling were the telephone operators. Branch control rooms were established in local schools. Puyallup's air raid watch tower operated continuously through the fall of 1943, with high reviews from the Pierce County Aircraft Warning Service and other air observation officials for its operations.[24]

New Western Defense Command dimout regulations went into effect up and down the West Coast on August 20, 1942, with all lighting that could be visible outdoors required to be turned off or blacked out.[25]

Instructions for dimouts were disseminated in the press, with this stern set of instructions appearing in the *Valley Tribune*: "Blinds must be pulled below the lowest light in your room this includes floor and table lamps. Porch lights must be shaded, likewise wood shed, basement and attic lights must not occasionally be turned on without proper shading." Dimout rules would be enforced more strictly starting on November 12, 1942, with warning cards sent to violators, followed by a fine for a second violation.[26] The maximum penalty for light violations was $10,000, three years in prison and banishment from the region.[27] Puget Sound Power and Light Company provided special light "hats" to the city to place on public lampposts.[28]

The 260th Anti-Aircraft Artillery Regiment

On December 9, 1941, two days after the Japanese attack on Pearl Harbor, the 260th Anti-Aircraft Artillery Regiment of the Washington, D.C. National Guard cut short its training at Fort Bliss, Texas, and boarded trains. "We didn't know where we were going," said Gunnery Sergeant Warren Eddy of Washington, D.C., who had joined the 260th Regiment one year earlier, just before it was called to active duty for training. "Finally we found out we were going to the Northwest."

Within a few days, the 260th found itself in Washington State, tasked with protecting it from Japanese air attacks. The 1st Battalion was assigned to Boeing Field and the Bremerton Naval Shipyard. The 2nd Battalion was assigned to guard the recently opened McChord Field. Without adequate housing for six hundred guardsmen at McChord, the battalion arranged to take over the Puyallup Fairgrounds while awaiting more permanent quarters. "It was the only place they could put [us]," said Eddy.[29]

Lieutenant Colonel Curt Hammond, a young second lieutenant in December 1941 and the last surviving officer from the 260th, recalled arriving at the train depot in Tacoma and immediately moving into the fairgrounds on December 13, 1941.

Not that the fairgrounds had proper accommodations. "We slept in our bedclothes on a cement floor in the horse pens," said Hammond.[30] According to Eddy, "You just lived wherever you and your fellow soldiers could find a place to lay down. I remember laying on one of the vegetable stands most of the time. The cold weather set in, and the pipes in the fairgrounds froze up. There was no running water, and the toilets weren't usable." Families who lived around the fairgrounds generously opened their homes for guardsmen to use their bathrooms.

Eddy carried his gun with him in downtown Puyallup. "Not knowing what the Japanese were going to hit next, we were always required to take our weapons with us with ammunition," he said.[31] The sight of uniformed, armed men must have been a strange phenomenon in the valley, the first visible sign that the war had come to Puyallup.

Christmas was also coming. Men like John Morris of Baltimore, who had just turned eighteen the month before, were a long way from home. He later described that holiday in Puyallup:

> *And then the citizens of Puyallup took over. [P]retty soon, cars were stopping at the main Guard Post (on Meridian) with cookies, cakes, pies, offers of dinner, pots of steaming coffee in their own coffee pots and on and on.... [C]ars would be lined up for half a block just to drop something off. And this was not just during daylight hours; many was the lonely sentry on the midnight to 4 a.m. watch that would have people stop by during their shift with hot coffee and a goodie.*
>
> *And as it got closer to Christmas we got so many invitations to Christmas dinner that we didn't have enough guys to fill the invitations. The primary reason for that was that we could only release ten percent of the unit at one time. That did not deter the wonderful people of Puyallup; we could only be gone for four hours at a time, therefore, on Christmas day, some families would have one group of guys at noon, and a second group at 5 p.m. Other families actually postponed their family dinners to another day to insure that they would get to have some of the youthful soldiers as guests.*[32]

Morris was the bugler for the battalion. Each morning that winter, Morris would climb to the top of the grandstand to play reveille and taps in the evening. As part of the 260th Band, Morris recalled marching up and down Fifth Street Southwest. It didn't take long for the children of Puyallup to notice the new band in town. "[W]e would have 20–30 kids and their dogs marching along with us," said Morris. "The dogs would be yapping and playing and the kids, girls and boys alike would skip along beside us in time to the music. Some of our older bandsmen must have presented a father figure to some of the kids, as they would play their horn with one hand and have a kid hanging on to the other."[33]

The 260th Anti-Aircraft Artillery Regiment, 2nd Battalion, remained in the fairgrounds for three months. Some guardsmen organized a basketball team. "We used to go to Puyallup High School and practice," said Eddy. "I remember playing the high school basketball team and we were soundly beaten because we were so badly out of shape."[34] In early March 1942, the men of 2nd Battalion moved to new barracks at McChord Field.[35]

Many of those stationed at McChord kept their ties to Puyallup throughout the war. The 260th Band provided entertainment for a dance in the Fruitland Grange hall one March evening in 1942. John Morris played the trumpet. That night, Morris met the woman he would marry: a Puyallup High School senior named Dorothy Heil. In May, Morris was transferred to Camp Hann, California, but he made a quick visit back to Puyallup in July for the wedding and returned to California with his bride.

"It was a big deal for all of us who lived in Puyallup that they were a part of Puyallup," said Dorothy Heil Morris. "Here they were far from home. It was all a new experience for them."[36]

Captured in the Philippines

On the other side of the Pacific, at about the same time as the Pearl Harbor attack, the Japanese launched an attack on the Philippines.

Carl Gabrielson, a Puyallup man who had worked in the shipping industry in Asia for American President Lines in the 1930s, had relocated to Manila after fleeing Yokohama, and he was there when the city came under siege. On January 2, Manila fell to the Japanese. Gabrielson was taken as a prisoner of war at the University of Santo Tomas. His father, Axel Gabrielson, in Puyallup first learned of his son's condition when he received a list of prisoners and found Carl's name on it.

Gabrielson took on the responsibility for insect and rodent control in the camp, working with the Manila Bureau of Health to maintain a high standard and earning praise for his good work. Although Gabrielson was fluent in Japanese, he refused to let his captors know it.[37]

Private Albert Tresch of the U.S. Army was also in the Philippines and taken as a POW. Tresch was the son of a Swiss immigrant dairy farmer. Al was responsible for more than his fair share of mischief in Puyallup in the 1930s. He was known to get in fights, he didn't do well in school, he was overweight and some kids called him "Fat Tresch."[38]

Eventually, Albert's parents sent him off to a military school in Oregon. After some time away at the school, Albert enlisted in the army on May 29, 1940. He was six-feet-two and 280 pounds when he was enlisted. He was assigned to the infantry and departed for service in the Philippines in

June 1941. From Manila, Tresch sent home a postcard with his photo in August. In the photo, Tresch looks right into the camera; he appears fit in his uniform, and he has a broad, happy smile on his face.[39]

Tresch was among the soldiers fighting to defend the island of Corregidor as the Japanese took over more and more of the Philippines. He learned to be resourceful to survive. "You ate monkeys and wild pigs. What you could catch," said Tresch. The troops had become malnourished by the spring of 1942.[40]

When American troops came under machine gun fire at Abucay Hacienda, Bataan, on January 18, 1942, Private Tresch and another young soldier put their lives at risk. They volunteered to go around the machine gun nest, where Tresch threw a grenade and followed up with his automatic rifle to take out the nest. They succeeded, but it came at a price.[41]

Tresch's fellow soldier lost his legs, and Tresch caught shrapnel in his skull. Medics weren't optimistic when they saw Tresch's grisly head wound, but they tried an unusual remedy. Rather than trying to extract the shrapnel, the medics applied maggots to the wound in the hope that they would consume the infected area. Every day for the next week, the medics cleaned the maggots out with peroxide before reapplying a new dose of maggots. "I would sit down and talk to people," said Tresch, "and they would hear them maggots. Chewing."[42]

Tresch improved quickly and returned to the fight. The *Puyallup Valley Tribune* carried word of Tresch's recovery on April 10. "With furious fighting now underway on the Bataan peninsula, Puyallup citizens know that Albert is right in the thick of the melee," reported the *Tribune*.[43]

But the Japanese continued to make gains. During the American retreat at Corregidor, Tresch was driving a half-track with his lieutenant as a passenger when it stalled over a ditch, not far from a bomb blast. A Japanese soldier emerged, his gun pointed at Tresch. "When I looked down that pistol I knew that was the end. Everything else was gravy," said Tresch.

In a moment when the two American soldiers' lives might have ended, Tresch greeted the Japanese soldier with a cheerful American "Good morning!"

"Good morning," came the amazing reply from Tresch's Japanese captor. Somehow, the greeting turned to small talk, and Tresch learned that the soldier had once lived in America. He was a graduate of the University of California–Riverside. Tresch told his captor that he came from Puyallup, Washington. As it turned out, the soldier had visited Puyallup once. He had gone to the fair. And now here stood this Japanese soldier face to face with a son of Puyallup whose life he might easily have taken. Indeed, he revealed that he had intended to kill Tresch and his lieutenant. "Every dog has got his day and my day was right there," said Tresch.

Having survived this encounter, Tresch and the junior officer were prisoners of war of the Empire of Japan. They were forced on a long walk to Camp O'Donnell in Capas, Luzon, a horrific journey known to history as the "Bataan Death March."

Japanese soldiers used their bayonets on captives who stumbled during the course of the march. "When you hit the ground they'd stab you," said Tresch. "That's why everybody tried to help everybody. When you're down, you're dead. So you had to learn not to trip."

Private Albert Tresch, 1941.
Courtesy of Lois and Cristi Williams.

Tresch's lieutenant, a man in his mid-twenties, was ailing early in the journey. "I [dragged] him as far as I could drag him and then the [Japanese] got mad and they bayoneted him. That was about two days out….The ones [who] made it through the third day, they lived. But the ones [who] were tired and all [worn] out to begin with, they gave up. It was more or less in their hands."

Japanese troops did not provide food to their POWs during the march. In his hunger, Tresch took the risk of stopping along the road to buy three boiled eggs from a Filipino farmer. As a consequence, a Japanese soldier stuck a bayonet into Tresch's hip. The tip of the bayonet broke off. "He ended up with a bayonet that wasn't sharp," Tresch would recall, "but I had the eggs." Tresch ate those eggs—his only food during the long march.

Tresch was not one to meekly submit to his captors. When he and a fellow soldier found themselves on a bridge with two Japanese soldiers, they managed to push the enemy troops off the side of the bridge. Tresch finally reached Camp O'Donnell on April 15, 1942. He would remember that date because it was his nineteenth birthday.[44]

It was in May that the Tresch family was told that Albert was Missing in Action. In the middle of June, the Tresches finally learned that Albert had been taken as a POW.[45]

Chapter 3

THE WAR COMES TO PUYALLUP

Everybody plunged into the war effort here," said Eunice Barth Gilliam, a 1942 Puyallup High School graduate. Gilliam did her part as the lead switchboard operator for Puyallup's telephone lines. She worked the phones six days a week, "and it sometimes ran together 12 days in a row, and then a couple days off, and by then you're so tired you couldn't see straight." She moved into a room at the Montgomery house on the corner of Fifth and Pioneer so she could walk to work at the telephone office.[1]

Before 1941 was over, the Marine Corps had set up a recruiting station in the Puyallup Post Office.[2] The American Legion aided with the general recruitment campaign, and in 1942, the Bruce Mercer Legion Post appointed U.S. Navy Reserve captain Fred Griffiths as the local recruiting chairman. Griffiths could be found at his desk in the chamber of commerce office at city hall every morning, answering questions and handing out literature for the service branches.[3] Although he may have been "a wee bit partial to the navy, his advice and information are free to youths interested in serving Uncle Sam in any branch," noted the *Puyallup Valley Tribune*.[4]

Frances Humiston, the wife of Lieutenant Leonard Humiston, worked on the nursing staff of Puyallup General Hospital.[5] Following America's entry into the war, civilian defense officials made it clear that Puyallup's hospital was a critical regional medical facility. Hospital owners Martha Lee and Edith Steiling and staff physicians Charles Aylen and Shirley Berry took swift action, converting a number of private rooms into wards, adding beds

Right: Eunice Barth, Puyallup High School class of 1942, Puyallup's lead telephone operator during the war. *Courtesy of Renne Gilliam.*

Below: Puyallup's telephone switchboard and its operators during the war. *Courtesy of Renne Gilliam.*

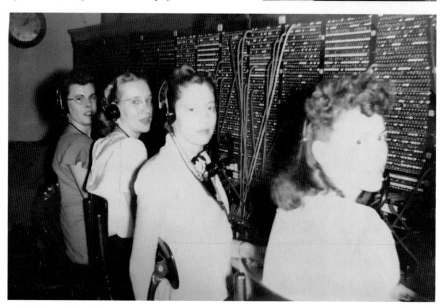

and cots and establishing a blackout system at the medical center at Fourth and Meridian in downtown Puyallup. Local builder and civic leader Steve Gray lent the hospital his portable gas-powered generator. The wartime Puyallup General Hospital would be ready for up to thirty patients at a time. As Martha Lee told the *Puyallup Valley Tribune*, "We are ready to handle any catastrophe which might occur in Puyallup."[6]

Puyallup citizens pitched in to help the Red Cross respond to catastrophes around the world. A local Red Cross drive early in the war raised $3,000,

Evelyn Keeney and Norma Lavorini take a class on airplane construction at Tacoma Vocational School in August 1942 in preparation for work in a Boeing factory. *Tacoma Public Library, Richards Studio Collection, D13340-2.*

with some downtown store employees donating a day's wage and Puyallup Valley Japanese Americans giving a total of $962.[7]

People from Puyallup—men and women—found jobs in war production industries, helping to make airplanes for Boeing or working on the Port of Tacoma tide flats. The Blue-Gray Bus Line expanded its service from Puyallup to Tacoma to accommodate various work shifts around the clock. The line gave priority to shipyard workers at peak hours.[8]

In the cause of wartime production, there was a sudden need for materials of all kinds, and everyone could do something to contribute to the effort. Local Boy Scouts participated in a paper recycling drive, collecting newspapers, magazines and any other paper people had on hand. Dr. Frank Killgore offered his house on Second Avenue Southeast to temporarily store the paper. Boys could earn their uniform fee and initiation by taking part in the paper drive. The Scouts set up a recruiting station at the chamber of commerce office to tout the incentives and grow their wartime movement.[9]

Women and youth work on a conveyor line in a Puyallup Valley packinghouse, 1943. *Tacoma Public Library, Richards Studio Collection, D156675.*

Over two weekends in April 1942, people could put scrap metals in their yards for collection; the chamber of commerce took a key role in coordinating the effort.[10]

The federal Office of Price Administration placed a ration on sugar, and sugar consumers had to register for special ration books. From May 4 through May 7, people in Puyallup could go to their nearest elementary school to sign up for ration books, with the requirement to report information about each person in their household as well as the existing amount of sugar in the house.[11] Other food products were rationed, as were household and automotive materials. Tires were rationed, and people had to get permits to purchase new tires.[12]

Gas stations collected scrap rubber that summer, calling on donors to give at least five pounds of rubber and staging a parade of oil trucks decked out in tires and other rubber items through downtown Puyallup.[13] A.G. Gross chaired Puyallup's Defense Salvage Committee, which organized a "Junk Rally Day" on Saturday, August 29, sponsored by Puyallup Valley

The Puyallup Kiwanis Club sponsored a Victory Garden program, August 1943. *On the ground, from left to right*: Fred Pyfer, Glen Cushing, Ruth Meredith, Gus Gross, L.M. Hatch, Floyd Wolberg, Henry Hansen and Cy Spear. *On the truck, from left to right*: Walt Vary, Gordon Bearse, Newell Hunt and Elwood Hunt. *Puyallup Kiwanis Club Collection.*

Chevrolet. People could drop off scrap metals, rubber, rope, fats, bags and other materials at the Kiwanis Parking Lot at Main and Third or at Puyallup Auto Wrecking Company, or they could call in for curbside pickup.[14]

The Office of Price Administration's price ceiling for meat led to shortages throughout the country. By the week of Monday, March 21, 1943, meat was scarce at Puyallup's grocery stores and butcher counters. J.P. Verone of City Market had little meat to offer, although he had some fish. Queen City Grocery shut its doors on Monday and Tuesday of that week but reopened on Wednesday with half a beef, three veal, sausage and fish. "George Greening, at the Puyallup Market, had taken off his apron and stood all dressed up and no place to go, and looked at the handful of fish he had left to sell," reported the *Puyallup Valley Tribune.*[15]

War bond and stamp campaigns were underway. Puyallup air raid chief warden Jim Brown headed a Victory Pledge drive for war bonds in the spring of 1942, with about five hundred volunteers assisting and recruiting friends and neighbors to make pledges.[16] Mike Barovic, owner of Puyallup's Liberty

AYLENS DONATE VALUED TROPHIES FROM FIRST WAR TO
SCRAP DRIVE
Puyallup Valley Tribune, October 30, 1942, 1.

Nothing but a major catastrophe like World War II could have
induced Dr. and Mrs. C.H. Aylen to part with two famous French
"75" guns, a German helmet, a British helmet with a significant
dent in it and a German sword which the doctor brought back as
souvenirs of his overseas experience in World War I. Now they are
part of the Aylens' donation to the scrap metal drive beginning
November 1.

War played a major part in the lives of Dr. and Mrs. Aylen,
for he was overseas last time with the Royal Army Medical
Corps, and Mrs. Aylen's experiences as a war nurse would make
interesting listening. The doctor collected the German helmet
in France, and it was there, too, that he narrowly escaped death
when a shrapnel fragment dented the British helmet he wore.
The sword he brought home from Germany after his service in
the army of occupation there....

This is not the largest part of Puyallup's scrap donation, but
certainly the most significant.

Theater and Roxy Theatre, took charge of the Pierce County Army/Navy
Relief drive-in theaters throughout the county. Puyallup was honored with
a Liberty Ship, the SS *Meeker*, named for Puyallup's pioneer founder, Ezra
Meeker. It was commissioned out of Portland late in the year. It would dock in
forty-four harbors during the course of the war.[17]

Women's organizations joined in the bond drives. Myrtle Renwick,
president of the Puyallup Business and Professional Women's Club, led the
local campaign during the national Women at War Week in November 1942.
Local businesswomen displayed posters to promote the drive, and Renwick
tracked statistics for women who were pitching in. Puyallup residents pledged
$262,534 for bonds in that drive.[18]

SERGEANT HOWARD JAYCOX

U.S. Army Air Corps sergeant Howard Jaycox was the first son of Puyallup to give his life in the war. Jaycox joined the army after high school and had been stationed in Alaska by 1941. He was a radio operator on a medium bomber seeking to take out Japanese naval targets in the Aleutian fight. Jaycox's plane took off on June 4, 1942, and the crew dropped a torpedo on a Japanese carrier but failed to sink it. The pilot, Captain Thornbrough, refueled the plane and "armed with bombs, took off again in angry pursuit," according to a story in *Collier's* magazine. "He was never seen again....A month later they found the nose-wheel of his plane, and the body of his radioman still strapped to his chair, on the beach some hundred miles up the north side of the peninsula."[19] That radioman was Sergeant Howard Jaycox of Puyallup. The army awarded Jaycox the Purple Heart and the Air Medal posthumously and presented them to his father, George, in 1943.[20]

WOMEN AT WAR

Many Puyallup women volunteered for military service. Restaurateur Doris Bushell moved to Puyallup after her husband, Chief Machinist's Mate Alvin Bushell, went down with the USS *Houston*, sunk by the Japanese at the Battle of Sunda Strait on March 1, 1942. Doris wanted to be "in the thick of things," she told the *Puyallup Press*, and wanted to keep herself busy, so she joined the Women's Army Auxiliary Corps. In November, Bushell became one of nine Washington State women chosen for the first WAAC officer class. She entered WAAC school at Fort Des Moines, Iowa, to become a training officer, helping to prepare soldiers for service in theater.[21]

Other young women enlisted in the navy's Women Accepted for Volunteer Emergency Service (WAVES), training at Hunter College in New York and serving in critical nursing and support roles. Seaman Second Class Clara Sicade, a member of the Puyallup Tribe and a Fife High School graduate, joined the WAVES and trained to be a navy shopkeeper. Seaman Second Class Marie Furin went into training at the naval hospital in San Diego.[22] Two sisters, Patricia and Eileen Ward, were commissioned into the Army Nursing Corps as second lieutenants.[23] Betty Gerstmann graduated from the Tacoma General Hospital nursing program in the summer of 1942 and received a commission as a second lieutenant in the Army Nurse Corps the following winter.[24]

Lieutenant Katharine Mussatto and Lieutenant Cleo McNulty, former members of the public nursing service in Puyallup, were stationed in India as army nurses.[25]

Women in service kept up long-distance relationships with their boyfriends in service. Private Laurie Otto, serving in the WAC in San Francisco, exchanged letters with her boyfriend, Machinist's Mate Third Class Norm Ward, in training at the Machinist Mate school in Wahpeton, North Dakota. "You said you wish you were home haying," Otto wrote on August 3, 1943, "say boy you aren't the only one. Just to be home haying and get married and have a house of our own can hardly wait for that day to come. I'll sure be glad when this darn war is over with....Remember we have a date after the war."[26]

FARMING IN WARTIME

Starting in February 1942, George Walker, L.M. Hatch and Rex Kelley headed a local committee on agricultural labor to conduct a census of available harvest labor throughout Pierce County, start a hiring program to recruit young harvesters and coordinate with government agencies on job posting and marketing.[27]

Fritzie Hermann holds up a box of raspberries she picked on the Hesketh farm near Puyallup in July 1942 as part of the YWCA Girl Reserves program, from the *Tacoma Times*, July 16, 1942. *Tacoma Public Library, Richards Studio Collection, D1306413.*

YWCA Girl Reserves berry pickers bring in berries from Puyallup Valley fields. The Girl Reserves allowed girls to help with the harvest, earn one dollar per crate of berries and live in pickers' housing while buying and preparing their own food during the summer. *Front row, from left to right*: Beverly Skaugset, Marie Reynolds, Esther Herrmann and Virginia Hermann. *Back row, from left to right*: Carolyn Lee, Janice Mechnik and Helen Harer. *Tacoma Public Library, Richards Studio Collection, D1306411.*

Janice Mechnik, Carolyn Lee, Marie Reynolds and Beverly Skaugset sit a log near the Puyallup River during the summer of 1942, when they picked berries as part of the YWCA Girl Reserves program. *Tacoma Public Library, Richards Studio Collection, D130648.*

Esther (*left*) and Virginia Herrmann picking raspberries on the Hesketh farm near Puyallup in the summer of 1942. *Tacoma Public Library, Richards Studio Collection, D130641.*

For one week in July, 150 men stationed at McChord Field drove out to the Puyallup Valley on their own time to work in the field and make extra money.[28] About 250 supervised patients from Western State Hospital in Lakewood came out to help.[29] Girl Scouts from Tacoma joined the effort. And on one day, July 21, 1942, six hundred local citizens dropped everything to go into the fields and do their part.[30]

In lieu of the Daffodil Festival in 1943, downtown merchants agreed to display daffodils in their windows in April. The Otto Reise bulb farm supplied flowers to the chamber of commerce to aid merchants in their floral arrangements.[31] And a group of Red Cross women volunteers organized a program to take convalescent soldiers from Fort Lewis on a tour of valley daffodil fields on April 15.[32]

Beginning in the spring of 1943, leaders of the Tacoma School District, Boy Scouts, Girl Scouts, the YMCA and other youth groups worked with the U.S. Employment Service's Puyallup office to lay plans for a youth work program to meet the needs of Puyallup Valley farmers during the summer

INTO THE FIELDS
Puyallup Valley Tribune, "More Workers Aid Harvest," July 23, 1942, 1.

There's lots of raspberry stained hands, yes and lips too, seen in downtown Puyallup today. This came about as the result when 600 valley folk composed of city officials, bankers, civic leaders, retailers, clerks, doctors, attorneys, waitresses, druggists, filling station attendants, members of the fourth estate and many others with varied occupations turned out enmasse early in the week to help in the vital berry harvest. Many of this group are still devoting every spare moment to the harvest.

Tuesday at 1:00 p.m. sharp, Puyallup closed shop and until five o'clock money couldn't be spent in the city. Doctors and druggists worked on farms where they could be reached by telephone in case of emergency. Slacks, overalls, straw hats and shorts was the order of the day. There was nothing spectacular about this event, there was a job to be done and these public spirited citizens were prepared to do their part in harvesting the valley's bread and butter crop. A truck equipped with loud speaking attachment rolled up and down the streets, directing people to spots where growers were waiting to take them to the berry farms. Once in the fields they joined some 80 soldiers from McChord field, girl scouts from Tacoma, bankers from Seattle, members of the state police force and hundreds of others from near and far.

Teens helped with the farm work in the Puyallup Valley in May 1942. *Museum of History and Industry, Seattle P.I. Collection, 1986.5.2909.1.*

Right: Women and children at work in a Puyallup Valley spinach field. By July 1943, more than 1,200 Pierce County youth had signed up for the Tacoma Chamber of Commerce's Agricultural Manpower Committee. A call also went out for 7,000 to 10,000 adult workers for the harvest of berries and peas in the first two weeks of July, according to the *Tacoma Times*, July 2, 1943. *Tacoma Public Library, Richards Studio Collection, D156679.*

Below: While much of the farm labor force was away at war, this boy and teenage girl helped with the Puyallup Valley spinach harvest in July 1943. Crates are labeled Kelley, Farquhar & Company, a Pacific Northwest packing company. *Tacoma Public Library, Richards Studio Collection, D156678.*

of 1943.[33] Farmers could register with the U.S. Employment Service by June 21 for the number of laborers needed.[34]

Farmers were desperate for help in 1943. Children and itinerant workers filled some of the need. On July 29, businesses throughout Puyallup shut their doors, and residents young and old went into the fields to help with the harvest, just as they had done in 1942.[35] The 1943 campaign for laborers saved an estimated 2,500 tons of beans from going to waste in the Puyallup and White River Valleys.[36]

PUYALLUP SCHOOLS IN WARTIME

To allow students to participate in the harvest through most of September 1942, Puyallup School District superintendent Paul Hanawalt announced that schools would start three weeks late. That year, school started on September 21.[37]

"This is the most crucial year in our history," Hanawalt said at the district's first faculty meeting in the fall of 1942. "Students are likely to accept this troubled state of affairs as normal times. It is up to teachers to guide our boys and girls out of this dangerous path of thought. The war cry of every student should be 'Lift up your eyes to the stars whence cometh help.'" Hanawalt added, "Look up—look out—look far; for he who keeps his eyes on the stars, can keep a twinkle in his eyes."[38]

At the first high school assembly that fall, Principal Harry Hansen said, "By cooperating with the government in every possible way and giving more serious thought to schoolwork, by eliminating all trivial foolishness, we can hope to obtain the final victory which is ours."[39] Affirming these things, high school newspaper editor-in-chief Lena DiMeo wrote in the *Hi-Life*, "PHS students have demonstrated a desire to cooperate in carrying out to the fullest extent the plans of their principal. To help the united cause, they are starting a scrap drive to salvage the much-needed metals. Yet they are continuing social activities with all the enthusiasm of the other years, reminding themselves that in spite of troubled skies, life is still beautiful and has something good to offer them. It is as if they have already realized the full meaning of Mr. Hanawalt's reasoning that 'the stars cannot be blacked out.'"[40]

School officials throughout the South Puget Sound region deliberated about what to do about high school football games in wartime. "Our athletic

Paul Hanawalt served as superintendent of the Puyallup School District from 1930 to 1960 and dominated civic life in the community for more than a generation. *Puyallup Kiwanis Club Collection.*

program faces a tough problem with night games ruled out and defense jobs occupying the day hours of the men and women who attend games," said Sumner School District superintendent Wade Calavan. School administrators met in Auburn to discuss the problem, and someone suggested holding the games on Sundays.[41]

On December 7, 1942, one year after the Pearl Harbor attack, students met to form a Puyallup High School chapter of the Victory Corps, the student organization of the U.S. Office of Education Wartime Commission. The club promoted physical fitness, participation in wartime activities and studies relevant to the "probable immediate and future usefulness of the war effort," according to the membership requirements.[42]

Two days after the anniversary, Washington governor Arthur Langlie spoke at a student assembly at Puyallup High School, calling on students to do their part in defense of freedom. "Liberty cannot be appreciated until we lose it, and then it is too late," he said. Langlie contrasted Hitler's regime of coercion with America's experiment in equality and opportunity. "The entire world is looking toward the United States for leadership and it is up to the students of today to lead the destiny of America tomorrow. In order to achieve this objective, all of us must realize what Uncle Sam means to us and then to strive to do everything in our power to make her better and stronger than ever. The responsibilities rest on your shoulders, and many lives may be jeopardized if you can't measure up to the problems facing you."[43]

On December 15, the local teacher's union met for a reception in the high school cafeteria and a discussion of the challenges to the teaching profession in wartime. Teachers missing that day included former football coach Al Dahlberg, a captain in the U.S. Army Air Corps; former band director Verne Jennings, serving in the navy; former junior high track coach William Gasser, a corporal in the army; and Louis Owens, an army private working at the Seattle Federal Building. Mark Whitman, who had represented his teaching colleagues in a recent Washington Education

HUMISTON SURVIVES AIR COMBAT OVER NEW GUINEA; AWARDED SILVER STAR
Puyallup Press, "Winner of Silver Star Citation for Gallantry to Spend Leave Here," November 27, 1942, 1.

[Lieutenant Leonard] Humiston was piloting a big Flying Fortress on a reconnaissance flight over a Jap base on New Guinea. A dozen Zero planes attacked the Seattle-made bomber and in the ensuing action, 200 cannon and machine gun bullets riddled, one motor and the ailerons were disabled and two members of the crew were injured. While his gunners were pouring 3,000 rounds of ammunition into the attacking Japs and shooting down at least one of the Zero planes, Lieut. Humiston was fighting grimly to get his crippled plane over the soaring Owen Stanley mountains. Flying blind and unable to bank his plane, Leonard finally succeeded in crossing the mountains and reaching the American base. There he was forced to groundloop, but the badly battered bomber sustained nothing more serious than a bent wheel."

Association conference, reported a statewide concern about teachers leaving for military service, which would result in a staff shortage for the next school year. Superintendent Hanawalt acknowledged the problem and encouraged school staff to work together to get through it. He urged collegiality and mutual understanding among everyone involved in the school. He said that teachers should get together for home parties, picnic outings and other social activities to sustain themselves as a faculty.[44]

CHRISTMAS 1942

Home on leave from the Pacific, Lieutenant Leonard Humiston joined the Bruce A. Mercer Post of the American Legion, becoming the first of the World War II generation to do so. A survivor of the first American air combat of the war during the attack on Pearl Harbor and a Silver Star recipient after a combat mission over New Guinea, Humiston received a hero's welcome at the 1942 Puyallup High School Alumni Assembly in the high school auditorium just before Christmas. Students entered the auditorium in a candlelight processional, heard Humiston and other alumni speak and listened to Christmas carols by the Meeker grade school chorus and performances by the high school orchestra.[45]

That Christmas, Victory Mail—or V-Mail, as it was known—was in high demand, and Puyallup postmaster Andrew Hunter told the *Puyallup Valley Tribune* that it would take priority over airmail in the event that space ran out. Customers could purchase a standardized letter and envelope, which the post office would scan and transmit to its destination on a small film.[46]

High school student Ken Turney worked at the post office. "At Christmas time, we worked long hours," he said. "We made every effort possible to make sure that letters from the servicemen personnel would reach their families here. Because this was important for the service people as well as the families. It was long hours, and there was a shortage of workers."[47]

Chapter 4

CAMP HARMONY

We're All Americans," declared the headline above a note by Mr. Harry Starbird, social science teacher, on the front page of the Puyallup High School *Hi-Life* on December 18, 1941. Mr. Starbird was a teacher who "made history come alive" and inspired many of his students to become teachers, said his student Frank Failor.[1] When he wrote for the *Hi-Life*, his wife had just given birth to baby Edward Starbird.[2] What did Harry Starbird have to say about the world after Pearl Harbor?

> *American entry into the war, with possible attack from two oceans and possibly from four continents, was a reluctant decision forced upon a nation that unquestionably preferred peace, and at the moment was engaged in peace conversations with Japan. With the great task ahead, and ultimate victory as our goal, it is well to remember those virtues that have made America a great nation, and which will sustain her in this hour of crisis.*
>
> *America is capable of straight-thinking; its aims are high, its leadership unfaltering. Certainly, ideals as faith, heritage, truth, charity, understanding and tolerance are not to be forgotten now.*
>
> *Loyalty of all citizens in this nation must be assumed if our goal is to be attained and we must grant that vigilance in war-time is absolutely necessary.*
>
> *Already, however, we see the need for tolerance and understanding toward those citizens of racial origin different from our own, who have contributed, as American citizens, much to American civilization. Let us not forget that*

Officers of the Puyallup Valley Japanese American Citizens League meet with Raymond West of the National Bank of Washington to invest money in defense bonds. Chapter President Satoru Sasaki and Lillian Mizukami are seated. *Standing, from left to right:* Tad Yoshida, Tadako Tamura, Betty Sato and Daizo Itami. From the *Tacoma Times*, August 7, 1941. *Tacoma Public Library, Richards Studio Collection, D117971.*

the road for these citizens of different racial origin at the present time is a rugged one—let us assist—let us understand.

America the "melting-pot" of the world, long a refuge for the oppressed of all nations, is a leader in a darkened world today, and it is a great nation only through the combined efforts of all its people, and the values they have adhered to throughout its history. Tolerance for all races and creeds is the basis for this greatness—let us not forget![3]

"ACCOMMODATIONS FOR 8,000"

Almost two months after the Pearl Harbor attack, on February 5, Major General Jay Benedict of Fort Douglas, Utah, sent a telegram to Washington governor Arthur Langlie asking for a survey of state, local and private facilities that could be used to house "evacuated enemy aliens and their families."[4] Langlie complied. On his list were the Golden Hop Yard in Toppenish, Longacres Racetrack in Renton and the Western Washington Fairgrounds in Puyallup. The army initiated further exploration on all three sites. In Toppenish, the army found suitable space for some 1,200 internees from central Washington. At Longacres, the army began planning to convert the racetrack to an assembly center for internees from the Seattle area, but few existing structures were available for housing on-site. They soon abandoned the site, but not before races had been cancelled from June 27 through Labor Day. And in Puyallup, the army found forty-three acres of grounds with forty-five buildings along with thirty-four acres of parking lots. It was thought that the fairgrounds could house 3,000 people and the parking lots could accommodate 5,000.[5]

Less than two weeks after the Benedict telegram, President Franklin D. Roosevelt issued Executive Order 9066 authorizing evacuation to military-administered relocation centers for anyone on the West Coast who was considered a national security threat.[6]

The federal government entered a lease agreement with the fair, with annual rent of $15,063 and access to forty-one out of the forty-five existing buildings on the grounds. A.E. Bartel, the fair's secretary and general manager, signed the lease late in March, thereafter assuring readers of the *Tacoma News Tribune* that the fair would be back in business by the fall of 1942. Private landowners around the fairgrounds also signed leases, giving the government the use of an additional five acres.[7]

Local residents debated the evacuation policy. Many business leaders were worried that the loss of Japanese American agricultural labor could harm the region's economy, and the Puyallup Chamber of Commerce took a stand against the evacuation policy.[8] Fred Griffiths proposed a resolution on the Japanese evacuation at the February 27 meeting of the Kiwanis Club.[9] "The Puyallup Kiwanis Club went on record at its meeting Thursday afternoon that the Japanese problem remain in the hands of the civil and military authorities where it now rests for its eventual solution," reported the *Tacoma News Tribune*. The resolution noted that "whereas great pressure is being sought and used to remove all people of Japanese origin from this district, together with others of alien enemy origin," the club has "complete confidence in the civil and military authorities, on whose judgment the execution of this removal rests, and we pledge ourselves to support our civil and military authorities in any action they may take." The resolution went on to say that "if the removal of any persons from our locality causes us hardship, we will pledge ourselves to withstand such hardships as a necessary burden to the successful prosecution of the war."[10]

On Saturday, March 28, General John DeWitt sent orders to the district engineer of the U.S. Army Corps of Engineers in Seattle: "Provide accommodations for 8,000 Japanese evacuees with necessary sanitary and messing facilities at Puyallup fair grounds and adjacent 34-acre parking lots. Completion date: April 15, 1942. MUST."[11] Site grading commenced that weekend. Then, on Monday, some 100 carpenters went to work at the fairgrounds. Even before architectural plans were ready for the new housing, the sounds of hammering filled the spring air. Hundreds more obtained work cards through the U.S. Employment Service and the Tacoma Building Trades. Just a week after the project started, 1,085 men were working eight-hour shifts. The work continued around the clock. When the muddy roads on the fairgrounds made passage difficult for trucks, horses were put to work transporting materials throughout the site. Otto Lunn served as resident engineer for the ambitious project.[12]

In the mud parking lots, family housing was hastily constructed. The buildings were twenty feet wide and long enough to accommodate multiple families in a single building. The floors were suspended just over the mud. The former parking lots were known as Areas A, B and C, with the fairgrounds itself known as Area D. Space under the fair grandstand was turned into 105 small apartments. Each area had its own mess halls, laundry facilities and bathrooms.[13] Barracks were constructed for an entire company of military police, and a one-hundred-bed hospital went up.[14]

"World War II landed in Puyallup with both feet this week with the establishment of an evacuation center for alien and American-born Japanese at the fair grounds," read the front page of the *Puyallup Valley Tribune* on April 3.[15]

Construction was finished on April 15 at midnight. It was less than three weeks after construction began and right on time for General DeWitt's deadline. The next week, the army dubbed the new facility "Camp Harmony."[16]

SAYING GOODBYE

The hastily constructed camp drew the outcry of the interfaith Fellowship of Reconciliation, whose secretary, A.J. Muste, caught the attention of federal officials after he wired President Roosevelt about the "EXCEEDINGLY BAD" facilities of the western assembly centers, "ESPECIALLY AT STATE FAIRGROUNDS AT PUYALLUP NEAR SEATTLE."[17] Colonel Karl Bendetson of the Wartime Civil Control Administration became defensive and insisted in a reply to Muste that all was in proper order.[18] Meanwhile, Pierce County's health director, Dr. Norman Magnuson, took issue with the poor sanitation of the new facilities on the fairgrounds, alleging at the end of April that sewage facilities had been improperly designed. Without appropriate treatment and disposal for sewage, the doubling of Puyallup's population in a matter of days posed "an extreme danger to community health," said Magnuson.[19]

As early as the first week of March, some valley farmers of Japanese descent decided to skip planting for the year. Knowing that they would need cash for other purposes in a time of uncertainty, farmers sought refunds on farming supplies.[20]

Many of the Puyallup Valley families who now faced evacuation were deeply rooted in the communities of the valley. They were the Mizukamis of Fife, who kept a greenhouse business for the farm community then known as Gardenville. They were the Uchidas, who farmed berries along the north bank of the river; the Egusas of the strawberry farm across from Riverside School; the Fujiis of Edgewood; and the Fujikedos of Sumner. They were the Yamajis, who came to Puyallup during the Depression and worked on the Turner Berry Farm growing raspberries, blackberries and strawberries.[21] They were the Watanabes of Firwood between Fife and Sumner. "Those were the days when strawberries tasted good," said John Watanabe, who was a sixteen-year-old Fife High School student when everything changed.[22]

It was baseball season at Fife High when the evacuation orders came. "When the evacuation happened, half of the baseball team disappeared," said Bob Mizukami, a 1940 Fife graduate. Coach Bill Vincent had to finish the season without several of his leading players.[23] "It was kind of a shock to us," said Mizukami, "because we didn't know that we would have to leave. We were born and raised in America. We were American citizens. We could understand our parents being interned, but evacuation should never have happened to anybody of American citizenship."[24]

Young Japanese Americans were not the only ones of their generation in the valley shocked by the evacuation. As student body president, Ruth Brackman opened the Puyallup High all-school assembly every Monday morning. One Monday in the spring of 1942 stands out among the others. From the seventh graders through the seniors, the students of PHS gathered to say goodbye to their Japanese American classmates. On stage, beneath the Viking ships that protruded from the upper walls of the auditorium sat

Right: Ruth Brackman, Puyallup High School class of 1942, served as student body president and presided over the assembly when the school said farewell to their Japanese American classmates. She later served as the school secretary, handling correspondence with PHS alumni serving around the world. *Courtesy of Sara Martinson Carlington.*

Below: A Fife Grade School class shortly before the war. Kaz Nakamura is circled in this photo from the Nakamura family's collection. *Courtesy of Kim Nakamura.*

Buses arrive at the Puyallup Assembly Center, where about eight thousand Japanese Americans were interned from April through September 1942. *Museum of History and Industry, 1986.5.6682.4.*

Puyallup's Nisei—club leaders, athletes, musicians and friends. It was to be their last moment among the Vikings.

"That was the biggest experience I had as a teenager," Ruth Brackman Martinson recalled.

Of all the opening speeches Ruth delivered during her year as student body president, "That was the most outstanding of all of them. I'm surprised I didn't cry," she said.[25]

Yukio Takeuchi said goodbye that day. "The hardest thing in my life is when we had to part from that stage," said Takeuchi's friend and basketball teammate Stanley Stemp. "He was in tears and I was crying because I liked him so well. We sat there and cried."[26]

Rosie Takemura was also among the departing. Rosie was one of the most popular students in the class of 1942. She and Ruth had bonded especially during their senior year, although the two girls along with Eunice Barth had often sat together at lunch since the beginning of their junior high days. Ruth was "very upset," Eunice Barth Gilliam recalled.

That certain members of the school should be removed on the basis of their race was bewildering to many students. "In those days," said Gilliam, "I don't know whether kids nowadays would believe this or not—but we were friends with everybody…Japanese, Filipinos, Indians were using our school the same as we did. We had no idea that people had such hate for one another anywhere else. And we were kind of isolated and protected. I didn't realize how much we were protected until I grew up."[27]

. . . .

AN OPEN LETTER TO THE PEOPLE OF PIERCE COUNTY
Puyallup Valley Tribune, *May 29, 1942, 1.*

To the People of Pierce County:
During the past several months, the realization has been ours that evacuation orders would come eventually, but most of us had gone through those days with the gold-tinted self-assurance that this evacuation was something in the distant future. But it has come upon us suddenly, rudely, and we awoke to the grim recognition that the order is not only upon us, but that the evacuation has already been completed for those of us in the Puyallup Valley. Of course we had been forewarned, and repeatedly; but still, we belong so completely in this, our Puyallup Valley; our roots so firmly implanted in the communities of the Valley....But now, we find ourselves established at the Assembly Centers in Puyallup.

The good people of the Valley are well acquainted with the members as well as the activities of the Puyallup Valley chapter of the Japanese American Citizen League....And we are certain that there is no need for us to tell this part of America that we too are Americans; that today, though actually "yanked" out of the only homes most of us have ever known in our lifetime, we cling with renewed faith to those ideals of America which have, until now, given us the initiative, the reassuring courage to establish ourselves so firmly in this American life. There is no need for us to tell America that the JACL is an institution of solid Americans: that the only "ism" with which we associate is that of Americanism. And we have made our substantial contribution toward this end in the Valley, and proudly....

And at this time, we don't believe it necessary for us to leave a message of farewell to this part of America. Our many Caucasian friends have bade us the most reassuring good byes "for the duration" coupled with the nostalgic expression of "until we meet again." The soil we worked, the soil our toil-worn parents worked so conscientiously—it has become too much a part of us to leave so easily. But since it must be so, we hope the Valley which was, and which is, our homes will continue to yield as richly with produce for America's vital food supply.

At this moment, our minds are a jumble of confused thoughts and emotions. What message can we leave with the American public? That we are Americans to the core—there is no need for us to assert the point. But we would like to leave a message of appreciation—a simply "thank you" from the depths of our hearts to this part of America for helping us to establish ourselves so firmly in this American life—so [firmly] indeed that this evacuation, no matter how hard it has hit us, our sense of "belonging" will remain as strongly extant. Our roots are planted too deeply in this, OUR America, and what lies beyond the pale of this, OUR America, we little know. But we do know that there is a war to be won; that the nation that gave us our parent generation is waging a ruthless war against us...that we must comply with the orders as cheerfully "as can be expected under the circumstances." But there is a grim determination with us that nothing shall rob us of this our sense of belonging in this, Our America.

Tadako Tamura, Corresponding Secretary
Puyallup Valley Chapter,
The Japanese American Citizens League

. . . .

EVACUATION

"By the middle of May, when the valley folks were sent to the assembly center, the telephone peas were waist high and strung, the pole beans were staked, early radishes and green onions were ready for the market, strawberries were starting to ripen and the lettuce had been transplanted," said Shigeo Wakamatsu long after the war. "Not much is known how the crops fared in the harvest nor what prices were obtained, but the Issei [Japanese American immigrant] farmers went into camp with their heads held high, knowing that they had done everything that was possible to help our nation face its first summer of World War II."[28] Wakamatsu said this in 1981 as he testified before the Commission on Wartime Relocation and Internment of Civilians.

But in May 1942, Shigeo was a student at the University of Puget Sound. Fellow student Frank Hanawalt told any audience that would listen the story of what it was like when his friend Shigeo had to leave campus that spring.[29]

As Puyallup residents said goodbye to their homes, farms and businesses, it fell to Judge Robert Campbell to keep an inventory of Japanese American property. To a large extent, the property was lost. "Their land was confiscated and some of their belongings sold to local citizens," said Campbell. "I'm afraid the Japanese lost most of what they had before they came to the camp."[30]

The first arrivals at Camp Harmony were 87 second-generation Japanese American Nikkei from Alaska on April 27. The next day, an advance group of 284 Nikkei checked in to begin preparing the camp for the much larger waves of internees who would follow them.[31] On May 5, 39 more Alaskan Nikkei arrived 5 during the week when 2,000 people from Seattle came down, mostly in buses, some in preauthorized private cars. "They moved by the hundreds," wrote Louis Fiset, "leaving the gathering points at nine in the morning and at two in the afternoon. After dropping their passengers at the end of their morning runs, drivers retraced their routes to Seattle to repeat the process in the afternoons. Transporting 1,137 Japanese-Americans on May 8 and 9 required thirty-two trips."[32]

Valley evacuees were ordered to report to Puyallup City Hall between May 12 and 16.[33] By the sixteenth, 3,500 more Seattle residents had left their homes and traveled south to Puyallup.[34] On that day, a Saturday, there were 7,376 men, women and children inside the grounds of the Western Washington Fair, about twice the usual population of Puyallup.[35]

It rained much of this time. The dirt paths among the makeshift housing rows became avenues of mud.[36]

Mito Kashiwagi and her mother-in-law, Y. Kashiwagi, hang curtains in their barracks at the Puyallup Assembly Center, called Camp Harmony, in this photo for the April 30, 1942 edition of the *Tacoma Times*. *Tacoma Public Library, Richards Studio Collection, D12804-6.*

Men construct their own furniture for barracks at the Puyallup Assembly Center. *Tacoma Public Library, Richards Studio Collection, D128044.*

LIFE AT CAMP HARMONY

"Of one thing I was sure," said Monica Itoi, twenty-two years old when she arrived at Camp Harmony. "The wire fence was real. I no longer had the right to walk out of it." Recalling that first night behind the wire fence, said Itoi, "I finally buried my face in my pillow to wipe out burning thoughts and snatch what sleep I could."[37]

The Nisei grew up quickly as they moved behind barbed wire, said Bob Mizukami. "I was a nineteen-year-old kid…the oldest son at that time, and the responsibility of helping with the evacuation was on my shoulders. When you're nineteen years old, you kind of grow up real fast."[38]

John Watanabe's youth was suddenly interrupted when evacuation orders reached Firwood. "I lost my ambition when they said we were going to go to camp. I thought it was like they were going to put us in an Indian reservation. I didn't think they were going to have military outside the gate. It wasn't a good feeling."[39]

Children playing at Camp Harmony. *Tacoma Public Library, Richards Studio Collection, D128043.*

Inside Camp Harmony. *Tacoma Public Library, Richards Studio Collection, D128041.*

Some five hundred visitors are said to have gathered each day outside of the Camp Harmony fence, hoping to say hello to a friend inside or simply to see for themselves what was happening on the other side.[40] Some wished they had stopped to talk. Monica Morash recalled walking by the fairgrounds as her friend Satoro Yamaguchi called out to her. "I didn't know what to do," she confessed. "I was embarrassed. I waved but I should have gone over and spoken to him."[41]

Leonard Humiston's sister, Gene, was in her junior year when some of her fellow PHS athletes were evacuated. "I went down to the Puyallup Fairgrounds, and we talked through the fence. I can remember talking with several. One gal was crying that day. 'I grew up here. My grandmother grew up here. Now they're taking us in.' Her grandmother died in that internment camp."[42]

Bob Ujick, a Puyallup High School student at the time, recalled one encounter at the fence. He was working at Bill Zillke's meat market downtown:

> We had a lot of Japanese customers that were in the concentration camp down there, and they allowed them one telephone call at a time....They would call us up and order up some meat....I had to deliver it down there....I'd walk up to the gate, and one of those stupid guards would shove a rifle in my face. "I'm delivering meat for Mr. So and So," I'd say. "We'll see what we can do. Leave the meat and we'll give it to them." "No dice. I won't leave the meat unless I can personally hand it to them." He was cussing and swearing. Finally, he went into his guard shack and got on the phone. The people who had ordered the stuff came to the gate and they handed me the money, and I handed them the meat and returned the money. Zillke said not to charge them anything, and he's sorry to see you locked up.[43]

Among the visitors to the camp were clergy of various faiths and denominations. Christ Episcopal Church rector Dr. Archie Sidders and Reverend Joseph Chester of Puyallup First Methodist Church led weekly Protestant services.[44]

Father Leopold Tibesar of Our Lady Queen of Martyrs Catholic Parish in Seattle, stayed in Puyallup and visited the camp daily.[45] Tibesar had ministered to a number of Japanese American families and youth before the war, and he made it clear to Bishop Gerald Shaughnessy of the Seattle Diocese that he wanted to support Roman Catholics in Camp Harmony however he could.[46] Father John Power, the pastor of Puyallup's All Saints Catholic Parish, invited Tibesar to stay in his rectory as he ministered to Catholics in Camp Harmony.[47] Tibesar began lodging with Father Power shortly thereafter, reporting back to the bishop that "Father Power has been most kind to me at Puyallup."[48] Bishop Shaughnessy wrote to Tibesar that Father Power "understands perfectly your situation and is very happy to be of some assistance in the sad circumstances that now surround you and your people."[49]

By the first week of June, 2,058 residents had received work assignments, with half assigned to food and lodging. There were barbers, shoe repairmen and clerks for the stores located in each of the camp areas. Other services were arranged by vendors outside the fairgrounds; for instance, laundry was sent out to local laundromats.[50]

"Summer's heat turned the shacks into bake ovens, for roofs of a single thickness of lumber and tarpaper provided little protection against the sun," wrote journalist Bill Hosokawa. "The partitions between units in most cases did not go up to the ceiling; a child wailing at one end of a 100-foot long

Some Japanese Americans at Camp Harmony played baseball to pass the time. *Tacoma Public Library, Richards Studio Collection, D128045.*

barracks disturbed everyone. Yet with remarkable fortitude the evacuees pitched in to make the best of their lot."[51]

There were deaths as well as births. Thirty-seven babies were born at Camp Harmony's clinics or at local hospitals.[52]

Internees produced content for the *Camp Harmony News-Letter*, which was published by *Puyallup Valley Tribune* editor Tom Montgomery.[53] A branch of the Puyallup Post Office was opened in Area D. Nearly 1,000 letters and around 270 parcels were handled in the post office every day. Because of Camp Harmony, the amount of daily mail arriving in Puyallup was more than twice what it had been before the internment.[54]

Sanitation concerns expressed by the Pierce County Health Department earlier in the year proved to be well founded. Internees dealt with overfilled septic tanks by hand-bailing the waste into trash cans, which were then taken to a landfill along the Puyallup River. In response, WCCA administrators directed a weekly hose-flush of the septic tanks, with the consequence of untreated waste flowing out and into the City of Puyallup sewer. Well beyond its capacity, the sewer drained its load into Meeker Ditch not far from Clark's Creek, and despite warning signs, local children were known to play in the ditch.[55] A committee of the Puyallup Chamber of Commerce called on city officials to seek federal aid for environmental cleanup.[56]

During the summer of 1942, Frank Hanawalt came home from college to Puyallup to organize a campaign to support Japanese Americans interned at Camp Harmony. He began by standing outside of the fairgrounds, where internees could see him through the fence, sending word through the camp to his close friends the Kajimuras. Soon, Frank developed a system whereby internees could place orders for drugstore items, always making transactions under the careful watch of a guard.

As Frank took orders and brought back the goods, other kinds of requests began to make their way to his attention. The Takehara family, having no way to bring sufficient furniture into the camp, asked Frank whether he could retrieve some of their furniture. The Takeharas provided the address of the person who was keeping their house key. Frank loaded the furniture into his car and transported it right through the gate of the fairgrounds and into the barracks area.

Frank was not universally supported in Puyallup, but his parents were quietly supportive, despite the protests of a few school district constituents whose complaints were registered in the superintendent's office.

Superintendent Paul Hanawalt made at least one public gesture of support for the Nisei students then removed from their schools. As Frank recalled, "He felt very deeply the injustice of the relocation action." Mr. Hanawalt went to camp administrators and requested a temporary leave for two Japanese American students of Puyallup High School who were to graduate with the class of 1942. His request was approved. On graduation day in June, the superintendent drove to the gates of the fairgrounds, where he picked up Rosie Takemura and Yukio Takeuchi and took them to the high school auditorium to walk with their class. When the exercises had finished, Rosie and Yukio made their way back out to Mr. Hanawalt's car, which he would drive back to the fairgrounds. But first, he made a detour up Pioneer and stopped at Martin's Confectionery. There he treated the new Viking alums to Mr. Martin's homemade ice cream.[57]

There were other stories of compassion in these days. When the Ota family left behind their farm, the Frye family next door cared for their property.[58] When valley daffodil farmers Ed and Grace Orton and their son, Stanly, said goodbye to Japanese American employees and friends, the Ortons took care of internees' land and made mortgage payments on behalf of landowners.[59] And when Lily Yamaguchi returned to Puyallup after the war, she found that a kind neighbor had kept her precious doll in safekeeping for her homecoming.[60]

THE TRAIN TO IDAHO

It was not until the first week in August that Camp Harmony superintendent J.J. McGovern officially learned that Camp Harmony internees would be transferred to Idaho. Earlier speculation among camp residents had focused on Tule Lake, California. McGovern selected 213 internees to travel on the first train to Minidoka Relocation Center to prepare the camp with food services, housing accommodations and medical services for waves of residents over the coming weeks.[61]

The train ride is an especially haunting memory for many of the Japanese Americans who lived through that time. One young Japanese American recalled with irony older children singing the popular song "Don't Fence Me In" on the train ride. Many who rode that train recalled the shades being down. The explanation for this is that military police on the train were concerned about public reactions when the trains passed through populated areas.[62]

Preparations to depart Camp Harmony. *Museum of History and Industry, Seattle P.I. Collection, PI28078.*

Sue Fujikedo, a 1939 Sumner High School graduate, recalled the long ride. "They pulled all the shades, so we didn't see anything until we got almost to Idaho. Then we could see sand on the banks. We were in a different place."[63]

A total of sixteen trains left the Puyallup station for Minidoka between August 9 and September 12. Two other trains departed for Tule Lake, California. Most of the trains bound for Minidoka carried about five hundred passengers in eleven passenger cars, two diners and two Pullman cars, with beds for small children, people with disabilities, the elderly and pregnant women. Leaving Puyallup, the train passed through Tacoma and on through southwest Washington, then through northern Oregon, southeast into Idaho and through Twin Falls until it stopped in Eden. Then the internees were transported six miles south to Minidoka. The journey took about thirty hours.[64]

Some internees had heard that the new location, as the name suggested, was like the Garden of Eden. But as Bob Mizukami remembered it, "We got

This train from Puyallup station carried Japanese Americans to the internment camp at Minidoka, Idaho. *Museum of History and Industry, Seattle P.I. Collection, pi28081.*

out there in the middle of the desert, and the train stopped and they said, 'Okay, get off.' There was nothing but sand and sagebrush out there....They picked us up on buses and hauled us into camp from there."[65]

The last train pulled out of Puyallup Station on September 12, 1942, with ninety-two patients who had been in the Camp Harmony hospital, along with their caregivers.[66]

McGovern was left with a small team of administrators whose job was to turn over the site to the army's 9th Service Command, based at Fort Lewis. The transition was completed on September 30. The command would use the grounds as a training facility.[67]

Even with strict dimout rules and the night darkness in Puyallup, giant floodlights over the fairgrounds shone brightly, and they became a matter of local controversy. "The brilliant lights at the evacuation camp have caused much comment and trouble for civilian defense officials here, who report that residents in that district do not see why they must put out their lights when they could read the paper on their front porch several blocks from the grounds by the brilliant lights," reported the *Puyallup Press*. But there was no dimout exception for these neighbors, said James Brown, the regional civilian defense commissioner.[68]

It wasn't until September 1943 that the government tore down the temporary housing units on the fairgrounds.[69]

MINIDOKA

In Idaho, the 964 internees from the Puyallup Valley and the 6,185 internees from Seattle settled into Minidoka as best they could. "They just scraped all the sagebrush off and built a camp there," said Mizukami. "Every time the wind blew there was a dust storm, you could hardly see across the street."[70]

Dirt would seep in through holes in the thin walls of the barracks or blow in around the windows. Mae Fujii of Milton recalled those dust storms amid the blockhouses and watchtowers. "The windows were not tight inside. We had a lot of dust inside the house."[71] One former internee set the scene:

The Yotsuuye family of Fife, following internment at Minidoka, Idaho. *Front row, left to right*: Elsie, Haruyuki, Sadao, Tommy and Kazue. *Back row, left to right*: Akinobu, Tadao, Mary and Toju "Tom." *Courtesy of Elsie Yotsuuye Taniguchi.*

"Mom used to come home from the bathroom with toilet paper....I'd see her making little wads and plugging up the holes so she wouldn't have to clean all the time."[72] Monica Sone saw a mother out in a storm and related it as follows: "A miniature tornado enveloped her and she disappeared from sight. A few seconds later when it cleared, I saw that she had been pulling a child behind her, shielding it with her skirt. The little girl suddenly sat down on the ground and hid her face in her lap. The mother ripped off her jacket, threw it over her daughter's head and flung herself against the wind, carrying the child. Someone pulled the two inside the mess hall."[73]

Internees lived with their families in cramped quarters, dining in large mess halls and organizing social activities such as Saturday dances. There was a school at Minidoka, through which 770 students passed. From the time the internees entered Minidoka, they were surrounded by an electrified barbed wire fence. Later, realizing that these measures were unnecessary, camp authorities de-electrified the fence and removed guards from the watchtowers.[74]

WORK, SERVICE, SACRIFICE

Internees were allowed to apply for work releases away from the camp if they could line up employment. "You had this helpless feeling, because if you did not like being in the camp what could you do?" asked Tom Takemura. Twenty-one-year-old Takemura and thirty other Nisei farmers from the Puyallup Valley were allowed to register for work passes in Chinook, Montana.[75] Bob Mizukami spent the fall of 1942 harvesting sugar beets and potatoes near Minidoka.[76]

Sue Fujikedo worked for an English couple in Twin Falls as a housekeeper and then found a job in a tomato cannery. Finally, she joined her sister in Salt Lake City, again working as a housekeeper.[77]

The Puyallup High School *Hi-Life* reported in November 1942 that most female Nisei classmates were living in the Minidoka compound, while the boys were mostly helping with the sugar beet harvest near the Montana-Canada border. "Now that the sugar-beet season is nearing an end it is expected that the boys will return to Minidoka although they have an opportunity to obtain jobs for themselves, mainly in Ohio and New York," said the *Hi-Life*. "At last reports, popular Rosie Takemura, a senior last year, is believed to have accepted employment in Chicago."[78]

Min Uchida, a 1940 Fife High School graduate, got out of the camp to work on a farm in Montana and then moved to Chicago, where he worked days for a soda pop maker and nights at a bowling alley. Then he volunteered for the army. He spent the rest of the war repairing army trucks in France and Germany.[79] All told, 211 Minidoka internees volunteered for military service, including 36 from Pierce County.[80]

All three Mizukami brothers—Bob, William and Frank—enlisted and served in the 442nd Infantry, an all-Japanese American regiment. All three had good reason to stay at Minidoka with their parents and two sisters, and all three volunteered. "Others may have said that they don't know whether they could go into the service with their parents in the concentration camp," said Bob. "We went in with a different purpose. We had to prove ourselves."

William, a quiet Fife High basketball player, was younger than Bob by one year and one day. When Bob left the internment camp for training at Fort Douglas, Utah, he instructed William to care for the family in his absence. "Well, he had other ideas about that," Bob recalled. It wasn't long before William abandoned his familial duties and met up with Bob in the infantry school at Camp Shelby, Mississippi.

The two brothers were assigned to the same company in the 522nd Field Artillery. They went ashore at Anzio, Italy, in June 1944 and fought through German-occupied territory below the Arno River. The fighting was intense. One night, about three weeks into the Italian campaign, the boys from Fife found a moment to chat. "Some of those shells are getting awfully close," said William. "Well," said Bob, "what do you want me to tell them when I get home?" No reply. They only laughed.

The next day, July 11, 1944, William paid the ultimate price for the country that had interned him in the Puyallup fairgrounds. "He was killed from a mortar shell," said Bob. "We were in the same company, but I didn't know about it until several hours later that evening. There was no break. They were stacking them up like cordwood. I really didn't spend that much time thinking about it. You see all that death all the time. It was another casualty, and that's about it."

The 442nd advanced through Italy into France, liberating Bruyeres in October and rescuing the Texas 36th Infantry Division, the "Lost Battalion," at the price of more than two hundred Japanese American lives. While Bob moved from a jeep to help clear a tree that had fallen across a road in the Vosges Mountains, a German mortar blasted the side of the road and sent shrapnel into his face. He was quickly bandaged and returned to his company.

The survivors spent the hard winter of 1944–45 defending Nice and then moved south back into Italy to conquer the Germans' Gothic Line. Bob and the 442nd had far more than their fair share of combat. "A lot of time we were considered cannon fodder, getting tough assignments," he said.[81]

Finally—even after the loss of one brother and the wounding of the other—Frank joined the Third Battalion of the 442nd late in 1944. He was aboard a ship bound for Italy when the war in Europe came to a victorious end.[82]

THE REMEMBER PEARL HARBOR LEAGUE

On December 17, 1944, the War Department announced that effective January 1, 1945, the prohibition of Japanese Americans on the West Coast would be ended.

Just because the evacuation was over didn't mean that the prejudices were. The Teamsters Union was outspoken in its opposition to the return of Japanese Americans to their old jobs.[83] Letters to the editor in the *Tacoma News Tribune* about Japanese American return were evenly split—forty-three in favor and forty-three opposed.[84] Puyallup had a few outspoken supporters of Japanese removal. Five Puyallup stores displayed anti–Japanese American signs in their windows.[85]

As the war unfolded, a local movement grew up in opposition to the return of people of Japanese descent to West Coast communities. The banner on page one of Nifty Garrett's weekly *Sumner Standard* read, "OUR OBJECTIVE: BANISH JAPS FOREVER FROM THE USA." Garrett's column on the editorial page echoed his slogan, and he wasn't alone in town. As the leader of the Sumner Homestead Branch of the Remember Pearl Harbor League, Garrett could boast sixty-five members. Founded north of Sumner in the town of Auburn, the Remember Pearl Harbor League opposed citizenship rights for Japanese immigrants, and in some cases, members proposed canceling rights for those who were already full citizens.

Garrett printed placards for businesses to display in their windows. "We Want No Japs Here. Hear," the placards declared. Businesses that posted the signs were advertised in a special "Honor Roll" below the "OBJECTIVE" on page one of the *Standard*. In addition, the Sumner Chamber of Commerce and the Sumner Rotary Club issued statements in opposition to Japanese resettlement after the war.[86]

Departing Camp Minidoka, January 1945. *From left to right*: Y.M. McLaughlin, Charles Kinoshita, Fred Kinoshita, Mary Kinoshita, Mrs. Fred Kinoshita, Jean Alexander and Reverend L.H. Tibesar. *Catholic Archdiocese of Seattle Collection.*

In Puyallup, local activists formed a Homestead of the Remember Pearl Harbor League, with Mrs. J.C. Williams as president and H.H. Reimers as secretary-treasurer.[87] The Puyallup Homestead sponsored a community meeting at the downtown Civic Auditorium on the evening of January 4, 1945.[88] Garrett led the meeting. After a number of speeches by pro-League attendees, R.S. Bixby, a defense worker, spoke up and alleged that the League was "cowardly, selfish, and guilty of fomenting racial hatred." Then an unnamed farmer spoke up and declared that "men of any race who were willing to risk their all and lay down their lives for the USA were good and loyal citizens."[89] To one observer who wrote to the editor of the *Valley Tribune*, it was clear that many in Puyallup were opposed to the work of the League.

. . . .

Camp Harmony

LETTER TO THE EDITOR
Puyallup Valley Tribune, *January 11, 1945, 4.*

Dear Sir:

Anent the mass meeting called by the "Remember Pearl Harbor League" in Puyallup, Jan. 4th. The call assured the public that speakers from the audience would be welcome. The chairman, C. Nifty Garrett outlined the aims and objectives of the League and reviewed its previous successful meetings at Kent, Auburn and Sumner where the mayors and superintendents of schools were present and gave their blessing to the League.

Mr. Garrett then pointed an accusing finger at the audience and demanded, "Where is your mayor? Where is your superintendent of schools?" Just where these gentlemen were at that particular time has not been ascertained, but they certainly were not there and the question still remains unanswered. These Puyallup officials seem to understand the nature of their duties very well indeed.

A long and imposing array of speakers were listened to. More than ample time was given to express their views; all favorable to the League. Then as the hour grew late a speaker in his working clothes and shipyard badge arose and broke the monotony by roundly denouncing the League as unchristian and un-American, warning the audience to beware of it and give no support. He was loudly booed, but also had his supporters.

The next speaker, a valley farmer, believed that men of any race who were willing to risk their all and lay down their lives for the USA were good and loyal citizens. He emphatically declared that these brown-skinned sons of American Democracy particularly picked out for attack were not only citizens by right of birth, but that they had proven their right on the field of battle and sealed it with their blood and their lives. The very suggestion to revoke their rights as American citizens was intolerable, and that they must be given equal protection and security beneath the folds of our flag as the constitution guarantees. This speaker was also unmercifully booed and denounced but was not without his supporters. Two other speakers spoke against the League demanding to know where the League was when they were on the picket line trying to prevent the shipment of scrap iron to Japan....

The crowd was well-packed with League adherents from outside communities and while League supporters did all the booing and made the most noise, at least half the audience of an estimated two hundred were with the opposition.

It is a safe assumption that Puyallup and vicinity will not be willing to repudiate the Declaration of Independence, the fourteenth and fifteenth amendments and all of our most cherished American Ideals.

I was there.

A.E. Applegate
Rt. 2, Box 120
Puyallup, Wash.

. . . .

Chapter 5

PUYALLUP GOES TO WAR, 1942–1944

You should hear some of the names [of military vehicles]*; some of them are really good. One of the best that we have is Little Joe with the St. Louis Blues. My own personal jeep is called Puyallup. You should hear the comments it causes. The biggest comment is, who or what is it, and how do you pronounce it. Yes sir, Puyallup is now on the map, that is as far as Africa is concerned. Chamber of Commerce please note.*
—Captain Stuart Van Slyke, letter to his parents from North Africa, March 24, 1943[1]

Seaman Second Class Vernon Brouillet grew up in Puyallup, attended St. Martin's College in Lacey and joined the navy in April 1941. The *Puyallup Valley Tribune* later quoted him telling his mother, Emily Czarnecki, when he enlisted, "Mother, look what this uniform represents. The most glorious nation in the world! We'll never let them come over here to bomb our homes and those we love. We're going there to get them. Every boy is determined to give them everything we've got."[2]

A crew member of the USS *New Orleans*, Brouillet was at Pearl Harbor during the Japanese attack. Thereafter, his mother told the *Puyallup Press*, "I haven't heard a word but I have a feeling in my heart everything is all right with my son. I feel God's will is stronger than ours. We can't win a war with tears. I'm proud of my son."[3] Brouillet survived, and *New Orleans* went on to the battles of the Coral Sea and Midway in 1942, as James Linn noted in his article "USS *New Orleans* Coconut Log Artifact" for the National World War II Museum website.

Mrs. Czarnecki received a nice letter from Vernon at her Puyallup home in November 1942. The next month, she got a Christmas gift from her son.

Not long after that came a Missing in Action notice. It was during the Battle of Tassafaronga on November 30, when *New Orleans* was severely damaged by a Japanese torpedo, that Brouillet lost his life.

Like other mothers whose sons were MIA, Emily Czarnecki had questions. So, she wrote to Chaplain H.M. Forgy of the USS *New Orleans*, who by then was famous throughout America for his actions and words during the Pearl Harbor attack: "Praise the Lord and pass the ammunition."

Chaplain Forgy wrote back to Mrs. Czarnecki on March 16, 1943:

My Dear Mrs. Czarnecki,

Your letter of January 9 concerning your son, Vern C. Brouillet, who is missing as a result of action of this ship against the enemy, has recently reached me.

May I be kind to you by being blunt and frank for I do not want you to be suffering longer than necessary with a most human and natural hope that your son may someday be found.

The term "Missing" as far as the navy is concerned means that the body has never been found. No man can be reported killed in action unless positive identification has been made. For there have been cases where men who were reported both missing and killed did eventually show up. However, the circumstances surrounding Vern Brouillet warranted no hope that he would ever be found.

We who saw the nature of the damage inflicted upon us are sure beyond a reasonable doubt that all men missing after the engagement died bravely and quickly. I am sure your son had little chance to suffer.

No personal effects were saved in the case of most of our men who were lost in this action....

Do not think that I am without feeling in writing this way to you, but from the many letters I receive from hopeful parents and friends I see I must be very plain in my language.

I too, knew your son. I was his chaplain. I admired and respected him. I am proud to have known him for in his hour of trial he proved himself a man and by his vicarious sacrifice he has helped secure our national safety, and make safe others sons and daughters of our land.

May you find in your hour of sorrow, peace and comfort through the Spirit of God, believing and looking forward to that day when 'there shall be no more tears' and that day when we shall be reunited in the eternal life yet to come.

Chaplain H.M. Forgy
U.S.N. [4]

Before his death, Brouillet made a pact with a fellow sailor named Irish Rawls that if just one of them were killed, the survivor would go to visit the parents of the deceased. So, the time came when Rawls went to see Vernon's parents in Puyallup. Brouillet left behind a girlfriend, Mildred "Mibs" Root, who graduated from PHS in 1943. Rawls met her, too, and they fell in love. They married and raised a family in Puyallup.[5]

OVER THE ATLANTIC

While millions of Americans went to serve in the Pacific in 1942 and 1943, others served in places like North Africa, the Mediterranean and England.

During the Sicilian campaign in the summer of 1943, PT boat commander Ensign Ed Jacobs was hit in the face by shrapnel. The date was July 29, especially memorable to Jacobs because it was his birthday. He received the Purple Heart the following week.[6] He was sent first to a military hospital and then home to Puyallup for a few weeks to recover. He was an honored guest of the Kiwanis Club in November, where he talked about his experiences in the Mediterranean. After Thanksgiving, Jacobs reported in to Bremerton Naval Shipyard for his next assignment.[7]

Ensign Ed Jacobs earned his Purple Heart as a PT boat captain in the Mediterranean in the summer of 1943. *Courtesy of Barbara Jacobs.*

Ensign Ed Jacobs. *Courtesy of Barbara Jacobs.*

Meanwhile, the air war over Germany was picking up. Air Corps staff sergeant Melvin Blanchard of Puyallup, a tailgunner in a Flying Fortress dubbed "Cabin in the Sky," was awarded the Distinguished Flying Cross for his role in a mission credited with shooting down at least eleven German fighters over Munster in November 1943. Blanchard was credited with downing at least two of the fighters.[8]

. . . .

A LETTER FROM PRIVATE FIRST CLASS FRED KUPFER IN
NORTH AFRICA
Puyallup Valley Tribune, September 2, 1943, 1, 8.
Kupfer was serving in an Army Engineer Battalion and
wrote this letter to his parents in Puyallup.

*We traveled about five days by truck and went to work on a
supply route going around Sebitala. We were there for a couple
of weeks when we moved again; this time another road job. We
got the road opened but not finished when we had to get out.*

*I understand that we just got out of there in time. All of
our equipment seemed to be moving back. We moved again
the following day, this time into a mountainous pass called
Kasserine pass. There we put out mine fields and took up a
defensive position.*

*On the evening of Feb. 18th the shooting started, the morning
of Feb. 19th, the battle started in earnest. The enemy were trying
to batter their way through the pass and they were strong. I
figure I was lucky to get through that day. On the afternoon of
Feb. 20th we had to withdraw. We got out what was left of us
and our tankbusters and artillery took over. The enemy must
have driven 15 miles through the pass before they were stopped.
We rested for a week and went back and buried our fellows.*

*Next we moved to Tebessa where we worked on roads and
then moved up between Gafsa and Sened where we worked
roads and pulled up minefields. It was here that our company
pulled up what is said to be the biggest minefield in North
Africa, 5700 in one field.*

*It's dangerous business with all their booby traps but not
too bad either if you take your time about it. We could sure
teach the boys in the states a lot more than they ever taught
us. We learned the hard way and lost some of our fellows at
it. Jerry planes kept us pinned pretty close to our foxholes after
dark with their flare bombs. We could lay in bed and tell the
difference between their planes and ours.*

*While we were at Gafsa I was with a detail of men picked
to clear the road of mines between Gafsa and Gabes. Here I
saw for the first time the British Eighth Army on its drive up
the coast. I only saw part of it and that was immense....*

Well, so we moved again. Never a dull moment; more roads to work on and waddies so build so our tanks could get through. Artillery was banging away over our heads all the time on this job. It's alright when the shots are going away from you but when you hear a German 88 start whining and everything blown up around, you wonder if your name is on one of them.

We moved again to where we are now, a town by the name of Mateur where we built stockades for the dirty devils who were coming in by the thousands. And so the war in North Africa came to a close....Wonder what now?...

Love, Fred

. . . .

PRIVATE JOHN HOLM

John Holm and his brother, George, left Portland, Oregon, and came to Puyallup with their mother during the Depression. It made financial sense then to live with their older sister, Tynni, who had married a grocer named Marty Martinson. They settled in at the house on Stewart Street. George finished up high school in Puyallup and graduated in 1938. John, a few years older, had graduated from high school in Portland and then panned for gold in Oregon, worked in a logging camp near Yelm and took a job at DuPont manufacturing gunpowder.[9] He sang in the choir at Immanuel Lutheran Church.[10] When the war came, John could have kept his job at DuPont—it was essential to the war effort.

Then John's girlfriend left him and married a soldier, "and that was the crowning blow," said his niece, Barbara Martinson Jensen. John Holm volunteered for the Marine Corps the next week.[11] He was assigned to the 16th Marine Corps Replacement Battalion, training in San Diego.

After Christmas 1942, John wrote home from San Diego about the meals: "All we got down here was a big dinner, and then for supper we went back to beans. We get them all three meals."[12]

On January 4, John was assigned to guard duty for a unique unit of Marines. He described it in his letter home: "Have to go on guard tonight at

Brothers George and John Holm near Mount Hood, Oregon, before they joined the military. John died at Tarawa, and George died after D-Day in France. *Courtesy of Barbara Martinson Jensen and Sara Carlington.*

12p.m. till 3a.m. tomorrow morning. Then at 9a.m. till noon. The only hitch to that is that my post will cover the area used for screw balls, guys who came in with prison records and odds and ends. Orders are to see that they stay in line and don't talk back. If they do make trouble, I have to knock their brains out. If I don't the Sergeant of the Guard will knock mine out."[13]

The next week, John's platoon moved on to rifle training. He described the daily routine: "Right after breakfast, about six we march out about two miles on the range and stay till eleven thirty. March back, have lunch. Back at twelve thirty, till four thirty. Back to camp, wash clothes take a shower

John Holm in his Marine Corps uniform. *Courtesy of Barbara Martinson Jensen and Sara Carlington.*

and shave. Supper at five thirty. Study from then until lights out at eight thirty." He noted that the food at rifle camp was especially disgusting: "I tho't that the base was bad! And no foolin', the stuff they feed us isn't fit for hogs."[14]

In February, John moved on for machine gun school at Camp Elliott, not far from San Diego. "Our whole platoon was busted up and scattered all over the country. Only about six of us here. It sure is a lot different than boot camp....It's going to be tougher, but at least you have some freedom."[15] The course at Camp Elliott was six to eight weeks, alongside only eleven other Marines. "It sure is a lot of brain work," John noted. "About a hundred and fifty parts to know the names of. We have to tear the gun down and put it back together again, know where each part goes, what it does, why it does it and what happens when it does it. This week we are going to take it apart and put it back blindfolded. My best time is four and a quarter minutes so far, without the blindfold."[16]

By March, the machine gun course had moved into the field to develop skills like determining distance for firing and camouflage on the battlefield. "We hide the guns and ourselves then we let the seargant [*sic*] find us. Just like hide and seek, only here we have to hide behind the smallest bushes. We don't do so much of that blind fold stuff anymore. We all know how to do that pretty good now."[17]

John's niece, Barbara, hoped that there was a way he could make it back to Puyallup before he shipped out. "As for coming home on leave, that's out!" he replied from Camp Elliott. "Couldn't get one if I tried. It's hard to get a fourty eight [*sic*] hour leave over the week end. Don't judge this outfit by the army and navy. They get a leave every time you turn around....Sure would like to get up there for a few days, but the only way I can do it is to go A.W.O.L. A fellow in our outfit just got thirty days on bread and water and fined fifty dollars for being over leave two days. Tell Barbara that I'm sorry."[18]

In early April, the 16th Marine Replacement Battalion shipped out for New Zealand. It trained for island invasion at a camp to the north of

Wellington known as McCay's Crossing. When John wrote home to his sister, Tynni, at the end of May, he reported favorably about the price of meat in comparison with San Diego, where "you had to pay a couple dollars for a steak dinner....Here, for as little as a quarter you can get one big enough to choke a horse."[19] Of course, John didn't say that he was in New Zealand or what the Marines were up to, but Tynni could gather from the letter that her brother was not in the middle of a war zone. He described the heat and the rain of the island as he sat writing home one rainy Sunday.[20] But when Tynni asked about the flora and fauna, he had to write back, "The birds are different. Can't tell you how tho cause you'll look it up in your natural history book or something and the censor wouldn't like that!"[21] His thoughts turned homeward to Seattle baseball, and then he imagined the Martinson clan driving out to a lake for the Fourth of July. On July 14, the Marines watched *To the Shores of Tripoli*. To Johnny, the movie was inspiring. "It almost made me want to sign up all over again," he wrote to Tynni.[22]

Eleanor Roosevelt visited the troops at Camp McKay, New Zealand. John saw her in camp as well as in Wellington, where the locals "think that she is quite the gal. They don't understand us when we call her by her first name tho!"[23]

In all the Pacific Theater, it seemed that nobody received so much mail as Johnny Holm. He joked that he came back from liberty one day and discovered that "they had to move out a couple bunks and the stove in our tent, to make room for my packages, papers and mail. Well, they would have if there had been any more."[24] It was almost all from the Martinson clan, including packs of Camels, a tobacco pouch, candy, valley strawberries, oranges, books, playing cards, a flashlight, issues of *Collier's* and *Life*, a stack of *Tacoma News Tribunes* and a stack of *Puyallup Valley Tribunes*.[25] "Several letters too," he replied.[26]

By September, there was little time to write home. "We spent three days and two nights playing Boy Scouts last week," he wrote. "As for spare time, anytime we get that call, we just crawl into our sack (bed to you)....In town I spend most of the time eating steak or anything else that gets in the way."[27] Later, he wrote that "there is nothing to do in town except fill up on steak and drop in to see a show....There [are] a couple places where we can get hamburgers tho'."[28]

If John, shy and reserved, was focused on the culinary side of Wellington, more than a few of his fellow Marines were interested in the romantic side. Many servicemen went to a club in the city for food, drink and shows. Often the Marines and the young women of Wellington just sat for hours talking

Private First Class John Holm at the beach in New Zealand. *Courtesy of Sara Martinson Carlington.*

about life in the South Pacific. John apparently warmed to the social scene as the weeks wore on.

One night at the club, Johnny met a local girl named Beryl Stewart. Beryl was a pretty New Zealander with a cheery smile four years his junior. And as Beryl described John, "He was a good looking fellow, tall and fair, being Finnish of course." She could tell that John was "a very quiet fellow." She recalled, "He didn't talk a great deal, but he talked a bit about his family." Beryl and John saw each other for dates several times over the next few weeks.[29]

Just before the 16th Battalion was scheduled to ship out, the Marines made a final outing to the city. They all wore their camouflage. That night, John and Beryl met for their last date on the town. They went to a movie, and when it was over, they said their farewells.[30]

As the time neared to ship out, John wrote home, "We haven't been doing a thing for the past week, except stand inspection, check equipment, fall out for roll call and police up our area. It gets pretty tiresome just waiting. From what I hear, we will be making a long trip."[31]

"Keep your chins up (you too Barbara)," he closed a letter on October 29. "Don't worry about me. Everything here, under control."[32]

"For John at Tarawa"

The Marine Corps invasion of Tarawa began on November 20. That's the day John Holm died.

Also, twenty-seven-year-old Private First Class Carol Lundrigan, a 1934 graduate of Puyallup High School who had been wounded a year earlier in the Battle of Guadalcanal, was struck down on the island.[33]

Don Henderson of Puyallup, stationed in Oahu with the navy, was standing on a dock at Pearl Harbor when he learned that John Holm was dead. Don knew John from when they worked together at Queen City Market. Now it was 1944, and as Henderson told it, "they were unloading seabags from the people who were killed at Tarawa. They'd have these big hemp slings with all the people's belongings in them. Just before this thing hit the ground, one of the lines broke and everything fell out onto the dock. One of these seabags broke open, and out tumbled a picture. I kind of went off to the side, and opened it up, and there was a picture of Johnny."[34]

John's possessions eventually made their way back to the Martinsons in Puyallup. "One thing that was very, very difficult when this was over with was the dribbling back of letters, possessions, wet clothes," said Barbara Martinson Jensen. "And Christmas packages that you'd sent. They sent back melted down fudge and cookies and stuff. And it just tore my mother especially. It hurt me really, really bad…but it just almost killed my mom. Another package, and then four or five days later or maybe another week or two weeks later there would be another one, and another one, and another one."[35]

John's fourth-grade teacher from Portland, Rachel Smith, wrote to the Martinsons with a poem entitled "For John at Tarawa." John and Miss Smith had corresponded just before his death, and he wrote to his sister asking to send flowers to Miss Smith for Christmas. It couldn't have been long after she received the flowers that she learned of John's sacrifice. "Soft waves break gently there / Trade winds sigh softly where / My John lies sleeping," the poem began. Miss Smith thought about the midday sun that would "shine bright and fair" over the vast Pacific before the night unveiled its stars—numerous, like the men who had given their lives there. She imagined their stars scattered in "Velvet skies… / Where hangs the Southern Cross." Indeed, "Many a heart feels keen the loss / Of other Johns like mine." But for Miss Smith, as well as for Beryl Stewart and the Martinson family back in Puyallup in 1943, "Our star—John's star / Shall shine eternally bright."[36]

"The Lord Was Pushing Me Down"

Back in New Zealand, John Holm had suspected that his nephew Del "Tiny" Martinson was somewhere not far from him in the South Pacific.[37]

As it turns out, Tiny was in Australia and then New Guinea, Papua New Guinea, Zamboga and Davao. Tiny "liked the Army," he said later. It was "a

Del Martinson on furlough in Puyallup with his girlfriend, Ruth Brackman. The couple was married shortly after Martinson returned from his service with the Marine Corps in the Pacific. *Courtesy of Sara Martinson Carlington.*

Del Martinson and a buddy in the South Pacific. *Courtesy of Sara Martinson Carlington.*

good life, except for being shot at." He recalled the "time I was within 6 inches of being killed. In the Philippines, we got ambushed by the Japanese, and I went down flat and heard popping above my head. It was bullets above my head. That was in Davao. I tried to get up but I couldn't get up. If I had gotten up, I would have been cut in half. The Lord was pushing me down." Two members of Martinson's company, including a close friend, were killed in that ambush.

Later on, also at Davao, Martinson had another close call when the Japanese dropped bombs near him. One bomb "landed about 200 yards from me, and a piece of shrapnel got me right in the side. I was a walking casualty. I looked down and saw blood on my shirt. I said, 'Man, there is a big lump.' Shrapnel had entered and left through my side."[38]

LIEUTENANT RICHARD "RED" SLOAT

Richard Sloat's student body president photo from the 1940 College of Puget Sound yearbook. *Courtesy of Mary Beaubien.*

One son of Puyallup, Richard Sloat, survived the Battle of Tarawa. Ed Bale of New Mexico, one of Sloat's commanding officers, called him "a fine, fine, fine man."[39] In the Battles of Tarawa and Saipan, Sloat was Bale's executive officer in C Company, 1st Corps Medium Tank Battalion. To the men of C Company, Dick was known as "Red" for his red hair. After Sloat assigned Doug Crotts of North Carolina as his corporal at Camp Pendleton, California, Crotts formed the opinion that "Sloat was one of the nicest [and most] gentlemanly people I've ever known."[40]

In high school, Dick was involved in drama and debate, but he was known to his peers in the Puyallup High School class of 1936 and to the surrounding classes as the preeminent student leader of their generation. Elected student body president in his senior year, he was a natural talent in school assemblies and speeches. "I think he would have to go down as one of the really outstanding students of Puyallup High School," said his friend Frank Hanawalt, who was three years younger than Dick and thought of him as a role model. "He was almost like an inspiration to me. I often thought in my younger years that he was going places."[41]

Following high school graduation, Dick studied at the College of Puget Sound, where he excelled in theater and speech and debate competition. "He would think on his feet and speak extemporaneously without having notes or having to think ahead of time," said Hanawalt, who matriculated at CPS in 1939, when Dick was in his senior year. By then, Dick was president of the college's student body.[42]

Graduating from CPS with high honors, Dick took a job as a speech and drama teacher at Kelso High School in southwest Washington. He taught there for two years. When the war came, he volunteered for the Marine Corps.[43] Following Officer Candidate School, Lieutenant Sloat was assigned as platoon leader with the 1ˢᵗ Corps Tank Battalion's C Company, in training at Camp Pendleton, California.[44] Each platoon had four tanks, and Lieutenant Sloat was the commander of his platoon's lead tank, an M4A2 Sherman dubbed "Cobra." There were four crewmen besides "Red": Corporal Buck Webb was the driver, Private First Class Jack Trent was the assistant driver, Private First Class Hank Trauernicht was the gunner and Corporal Bill Eads was the radioman.[45] Lieutenant Sloat earned both the respect and friendship of his "Cobra" crew. "He was real easy to get along with," said Corporal Eads of Salinas, California. "Everybody liked him."[46]

On July 19, 1943, 1ˢᵗ Corps shipped out of San Diego aboard the USS *Ashland*, cruising thirty-one days to New Caledonia. There the men drilled and waited for three months. In November, the tankers re-boarded the *Ashland* and joined an armada northward to Tarawa.[47]

C Company loaded into landing crafts to join the third wave. Unable to traverse a reef hundreds of yards from a landing zone called Betio, the landing craft carrying "Cobra" deposited its tanks onto the reef. They plowed their way onto the beach, littered with casualties from the first and second waves. And then they drove on through what Corporal Eads described as "random" shooting.[48]

Most of C Company's fourteen tanks were disabled in the first day of the fight at Betio.[49] "Cobra" defied the odds and tracked to the edge of a Japanese airstrip by nightfall, where the crew rested.

Early on the second day, Corporal Webb got under the tank through a trapdoor, probably to check up on a maintenance issue. A Japanese sniper was watching. Webb took a fatal bullet. As "Buck" lay dying in the "Cobra," Lieutenant Sloat administered morphine.[50]

Private First Class Trent took over as driver. Through the morning and early afternoon, "Cobra" launched 75mm shells at targets around the airstrip. Then Lieutenant Sloat received orders back to the beachhead at "Red Beach One" to take out a Japanese gun emplacement along the seawall. He directed the tank out along the carnage-laden beach and into shallow water to fire on the enemy.

As "Cobra" approached its line of fire, with the Japanese guns overhead training for an exchange, the Sherman suddenly tipped onto its side in a massive shell crater. Machine gun fire exploded from the seawall, but now water was seeping into the helpless tank, and the crew compartment was filling up. The four Marines had no choice but to bail out through a rear hatch and slide into the water, hoping to evade the machine guns.[51]

Corporal Eads described what happened next. "I had gotten out of the tank and was swimming towards an area that looked like it might be safe, and I got hit by a .50 caliber in the water. I think it was a .50 caliber—it was a big enough hole." Trent was also wounded in the water, and he and Eads regrouped on the beach to locate a medic. They were evacuated to a hospital ship bound for Hawaii.

As for the redheaded lieutenant from Puyallup, he apparently made it to shore without a scratch. He survived Tarawa, and the battle concluded two days later.[52]

To this day, the "Cobra" sits in the haunted waters off Red Beach One.[53]

PUYALLUP STEPS UP FOR WAR BONDS

In the summer and fall of 1943, civic boosters led by Frank Bates challenged friends, neighbors and coworkers to invest in war bonds for Puyallup's third war loan drive. The goal: $1 million. Pledges grew with strong encouragement from both the business and labor sectors. Oscar Williams rallied members of the Cannery Workers Union. Cletus Tegner enlisted the Saw Mill Workers. The Western Washington Fair Association board had invested $65,000 in war bonds by the fall of 1943. In early October, Bates announced that people in Puyallup had committed more than $1 million to the bond campaign, exceeding the city's quota.[54]

For the next bond drive that winter, 4-H member Marge Tallada of Riverside emerged as Pierce County's top 4-H bond seller, an important distinction in the 4-H's campaign to raise enough commitments to pay for a Liberty Ship.[55]

THE FIGHT FOR SAIPAN

Following the fight for Tarawa, C Company, 1st Corps Medium Tank Battalion shipped to Hawaii, where Lieutenant Sloat trained with his men for the landing at Saipan.

"As a platoon leader, he was probably the best I have had," said Ed Bale, Sloat's company commander and later a career Marine Corps officer. "He understood what he had to do, and he did it.…You were always sure that he either understood an order or he asked for clarification. You knew it was going to be executed in the best manner possible."[56]

In Hawaii, Bale named Sloat as C Company's executive officer. Although Sloat preferred the role of tank platoon commander, Bale realized that he couldn't do without Sloat as his second in command. Sloat was "so different because he had an enthusiasm about him that you didn't find in a lot of lieutenants in those days, simply because they were in the Marine Corps to avoid being drafted in the Army," said Bale. "They would do the minimum expected, where he would always go all out in anything he did."

While other officers spent evenings at the Kona Inn or weekends at Hilo, according to Bale, "Red pretty well stayed around, and he would take the duties so other people could go, because we always had to leave one officer in charge of whatever troops were there."

For the Battle of Saipan, Sloat was assigned to organize the transport of supplies to where Bale and the rest of C Company were positioned on the side of Mount Tapochau. After the 2nd Marine Division's initial landing at Saipan on June 15, 1944, Sloat stayed on board a tank landing ship with supply troops for two days before starting their supply runs. Through the rest of June and into July, he traveled back and forth from the landing area to Mount Tapochau and other parts of the island.[57]

. . . .

A Letter from Lieutenant Dick Sloat, Saipan, July 5, 1944, Gary Whitley Collection.

Aunt Gladys, Uncle Dan, Shirley and all the Whitleys,
…I'm writing under a tarp set up in the yard of some Jap farmer's place on Saipan island so you'll have to excuse all errors, etc. It has been 20 days since we have been away from the sound of gun fire and we all are getting a little off the beam. I managed to get in the assault waves again so have seen quite a bit of the "fun.".…I often think of you and hope you are all well. We are working hard at our job here and hope it is soon over. We have a long way to go yet however. Say

hello to everyone, and thanks again for the Xmas gift. It was thoughtful of you. Bye.

Dick

. . . .

On July 7, a few days after the Marines' Fourth of July attack on the Harbor of Saipan, Lieutenant Gerald English of the 4th Tank Battalion, fearing land mines in his area of advance, called for engineers to clear the roadway ahead of him. Bale learned of English's request. Since some of C Company's men had been in the area just hours earlier, Bale was certain that the road was free of mines, and he intended to relay the message to English personally.

Then Sloat volunteered to help. "It was my job to go," said Bale. "I didn't go simply because he wanted to go so bad. And he was that kind of officer. I've had lieutenants that I've had to fire in combat. He was very different. He was very devoted to duty. You could rely on him. You didn't have to tell him but once. He was always pleasant and enthusiastic, even under the worst of circumstances."

Sloat made his way into the valley below, talking by tank phone along the way to Corporal Eads. When he reached the 4th Tank Battalion's area, he located Lieutenant English's tank. Sloat picked up the tank phone. It wasn't working. He crawled onto the tank to make contact with someone inside. But a Japanese gunman was watching. The gunman fired a direct shot into Sloat. A few men helped to carry his body back up the hill. That July day, Ed Bale learned that Sloat was dead.[58]

The news of Sloat's sacrifice weighed heavily on Puyallup. "It seemed like a big loss when he was killed, because he was an outstanding person," said Betty Porter Dunbar, who was a year behind Sloat at PHS. On a landing ship medium in the Pacific, Frank Hanawalt received a letter from his mother. "When I heard about his being killed on Saipan—that to me was a great loss," he said.[59]

Red Sloat wasn't the only son of Puyallup to give his life at Saipan. Private Leonard Birdwell, who had grown up in Puyallup and worked as a logger before entering the service, was killed in action on the Fourth of July. Five days later, Private First Class Elmer Bottke of South Hill died in the final moments of the battle.[60]

PRIVATE GLASER AND PRIVATE RINKER

Private Roy Rinker of Ohio first met Private Ray Glaser of Puyallup in training at Chico, California. Both men received assignments to work in a new U.S. Army Air Corps aerial machine gun training program at Kingman Army Air Base in Arizona. Roy, Ray and two other soldiers shared the car ride from Chico to Kingman in January 1943. "He and I both wound up somehow with office jobs in the same office," said Rinker. Ray worked in the personnel section. The two young men lodged in "a big two story barracks that had two rooms at either end of each barracks. I guess they were meant to be for upper personnel for somebody to look over all the guys. They weren't using anybody in that respect, so they just opened them up to guys who were on the main floor. Ray and I happened to end up in the same room. I became pretty close to him because of that."

Ray was enjoyable to be around. "He was a fun, cutup guy," said Rinker. "He liked to joke and kid and tease. He had his serious side too."

Rinker recalled the nights of fellowship in that barracks hall at Kingman. "His bunk was over here and mine was over here and we'd talk every night like people do," said Rinker. "He apparently didn't have a girlfriend when he left Puyallup. He didn't talk too much about girls. I think he said he had a car—he had acquired an old junker shortly before he went in the service, but left it [at home]."

Ray often talked about Puyallup. "Ray was pretty young, younger than I, fresh out of home, which meant a lot to him yet, so that's what he talked about a lot," said Rinker. Ray talked a lot about Puyallup High School, where he had graduated in 1941. "Ray wasn't that long out of high school, and he referred a lot to his school activities," Rinker added. Ray had been president of the PHS Hi-Yi club and a member of the glee club, and he headed the costume committee for school operettas. "He was a little guy.... [H]e didn't participate in sports, but I got the idea that he was pretty popular around school."

In 1943, some Northwest airmen stationed at bases in California and the Southwest returned home for Christmas by way of McChord Field. One was Ray Glaser. "We'll see you soon," his buddy Roy Rinker recalled telling him as he departed Kingman Army Air Base before Christmas. "We expected him back."[61]

After an enjoyable time with family over the holiday, Glaser hopped aboard a Flying Fortress out of McChord to fly back to Los Angeles on the morning of January 2, 1944. There were fourteen men on board. Not far from McClellan Field in Sacramento, the plane exploded in midair, killing thirteen of the fourteen men—one man escaped in his parachute.[62]

Airmen from McChord Field served as pallbearers for Glaser's memorial service at All Saints Catholic Church.[63]

Roy Rinker kept in touch with a U.S. Air Corps friend in Seattle following the war. On a visit to his Seattle friend in 1946, Rinker made a stop in Puyallup to meet Ray's parents. Ray's death a few years earlier was "a pretty sorrowful event for them yet when I came there," he recalled. The Glasers invited Rinker to stay with them, but he insisted on staying in a Puyallup motel instead. "I ended up staying two weeks," he recalled. While he was in Puyallup, he met a young woman named Sheila. They started dating. Roy decided he'd stay in the Northwest, and he found a job in the chemistry lab of the Western Washington Experiment Station. Roy and Sheila were married several months later, and they lived in Puyallup the rest of their lives.[64]

Puyallup Women Proud of Record
Agnes Montgomery, *Puyallup Valley Tribune*, March 2, 1944, 6.

Puyallup women have taken the work of the Red Cross in its various departments much to themselves. They are putting in long hours cutting and making garments for men in hospitals, clothing for refugees in the stricken countries of Europe, and in making surgical dressings for the wounded on battle fields and in hospitals all over the world.

Methodist and Presbyterian women took the initiative step in January of 1940 carrying on for two years. The work is now sponsored by the Puyallup Coordinating council. The building in which cutting is done is donated by the Methodist church....

Mrs. Newell Hunt has been Puyallup chairman since the beginning, with Mrs. Roy Goodner as assistant. Mrs. Floyd Chase is in charge of distribution and receiving records, and Mrs. William Pence takes care of publicity. Finished garments are returned to the Tacoma station.

Garments made for refugees for men, women and children total 471 and include underwear, dresses, night wear, shirts, convalescent robes (for men in hospitals) hospital slippers and baby quilts.

Knitted garments for men in service include knee, ankle, bed and stump socks (the latter for amputated limbs), sweaters, caps, helmets, gloves and caps, totaling 192 knit pieces.

This work has involved approximately 325 women in the finishing, and 68 women in eight different societies, a month in cutting rooms. Women of Puyallup and surrounding areas have taken the work home to complete. The work is done by volunteers who are credited with 4,500 hours from October 1943 to February 18, 1944.

Much as the garments for refugees are needed, there is increased call for surgical dressings. This work is carried on in Sumner since Puyallup has no suitable place. Mrs. Stanley Staatz is Pierce county chairman for places outside Tacoma. Puyallup women have taken up this work in earnest, going over Wednesdays, Fridays, Thursday, and Thursday evenings. Approximately 100 women a week gather in the rooms over the Sumner fire station for this work.

The making of surgical dressings was begun in January 1941. After Pearl Harbor the work was taken up more seriously. In 1942–'43, 158,823 bandages were made. In January of this year, the number was 17,017 as compared with 4,143 the previous year.

Supervisors from Puyallup include Miss Anna Brand who is at hand whenever the rooms are open. In point of hours she has the most. Others from here in point of service are Mrs. Burr Gregory, Mrs. J.W. Kemp, Mrs. Pierce Levitt, Mrs. Meade Murray, Mrs. Steve Gray, Mrs. H.D. Barto and Mrs. Emmett Burks.

Women are urged to come to the bandage rooms to help in the making of bandages. We are told the greatest battles are yet to come. Dressings will be most necessary. A few hours a day in the bandage room may mean life or death to some man in service.

PRAYERS FOR SERVICE MEMBERS

Jack Barker, who was a teenager during the war and later became a pastor, recalled Sunday services led by Reverend Clive Taylor at Puyallup First Christian Church. "Every Sunday morning he would pray for every division, regiment, and squadron in the army, navy, Coast Guard, Marines, etc. We high school students got a kick out of that. He didn't want to miss anybody."[65] Taylor conducted the service for Aviation Radio Technician Second Class Gordon Heckendorn on April 13. Newly married before he left for service in the Pacific in 1943, Heckendorn's plane crashed in the Pacific near the Kurile Islands in the spring of 1944.[66]

HOMETOWN FRIENDS

Ensign Frank Hanawalt. *Courtesy of Bill Hanawalt.*

Costly as the war was, there were moments when people from Puyallup felt the power of friendship and grace, often as they learned how small the world is.

Chuck Krippahne, a 1937 PHS grad, joined the war in North Africa. "We landed in North Africa by boat, and I got in a cab," he said. "The driver asked where I was from. 'Puyallup,' I said. 'I am too!' he said." Later on, Krippahne was a tentmate with Dick Warren, a neighbor who grew up near Krippahne not far from All Saints Church.[67]

And there was the time when Frank Hanawalt came across his friend from Puyallup Frank Failor in the South Pacific. One day, on his destroyer escort in Lingayan Cove off New Guinea, Hanawalt learned that a landing ship medium, *LSM-27*, was nearby in that cove. He knew that his best friend from high school, Frank Failor, was serving on that ship. "So I went up to our signal deck and had our signalman send a message to Frank Failor, and our communication then was mostly blinker, and here came the message back from Frank Failor,"

Frank Hanawalt in China during the postwar reoccupation, probably December 1945. *Courtesy of Bill Hanawalt.*

said Hanawalt. "That night he visited our ship and I invited him to dinner and he invited me to his ship for dinner the next night." Failor recalled that they used pressed linen and ate canned turkey. So it was that two friends found each other and dined together in the midst of the war in the South Pacific.[68]

Chapter 6

D-DAY AND BEYOND

We believe when D-Day comes, it will be like the outburst of some great cataclysm, when echoes are heard around the earth. D-Day opens the second front.... We, living so far away, can only hope and pray—that Heaven will be with the landing armies of the Allies when D-Day comes, and that the victory will come swiftly and surely to our forces over there.
—Puyallup Valley Tribune,
"D-Day; H-Hour," editorial, May 25, 1944

When John Holm was killed at Tarawa, his brother, George, was in infantry training with the army. For some reason, George was disqualified from military service on his first attempt. "About George," John had written home from basic training at San Diego on hearing the report, "don't tell him, but I'm glad to hear that he didn't get in. It's no place for kids, anyway! Don't know what I'm doing in here myself."[1] On his second attempt, sometime early in 1943, George was able to enlist in the army. He quickly got married to his sweetheart in a small ceremony in front of the fireplace at the family house at 721 Stewart; Reverend Brackman of the Lutheran church was the officiant.[2]

That spring, George was in basic training at Camp Robinson, Arkansas. When the Arkansas River flooded in May, the army was called in from Camp Robinson to orchestrate the rescue work. "The Arkansas river is on rampage (the worst flood in over 100 years), and us poor soldiers have to go down + take care of it," George wrote to his sister just before heading out, fully packed with a week's clothing.[3]

Later, in infantry training in Texas, "He almost starved to death because of the bugs," said his niece, Barbara Martinson Jensen. "He couldn't eat Texas food because of the little things in the bread, little things in the cereal. And he couldn't eat anything. They put him in the hospital and had to force-feed him."

Then, in the spring of 1944, Private George Holm was in England, among the thousands of Allied servicemen readying for the crossing of the English Channel and the invasion of German-occupied France.[4]

Private First Class George Holm.
Courtesy of Sara Martinson Carlington.

LIEUTENANT RAY BOTSFORD

In the lead-up to the invasion, the little rural community of South Hill was shaken when First Lieutenant Ray Botsford of Puyallup Heights lost his life in a Thunderbolt plane crash in England on May 2, 1944. The 1939 Puyallup High School graduate was remembered for his talent on the violin. His classmate Earl White recalled, "Ray and I played the violin for a long time until my folks got tired of my violin strings breaking. Most of them were intentional to get out of practicing."[5] But Ray put in his practice and kept it up. Botsford was "a good violinist," said Essey Kinsey Faris. He played in the Puyallup High School orchestra, along with Barney Stemp, Bob Aylen and Dean McCurdy in the violin section.[6] Faris recalled Botsford, Stemp and Aylen as a violin trio playing "Sleep, Sleep, Sleep" on one occasion. "And it put me to sleep," she said.[7]

Botsford pursued musical studies at the University of Washington before the war came. He had been commissioned and received his wings in March 1943. He had flown a number of combat missions over Europe. He was about to get married to his sweetheart, Jean Kemp. Ray and his brother, Sergeant Bernie Botsford, had both been in England, Bernie as a B-25 tailgunner.[8]

JUNE 6, 1944

In the hours before the amphibious invasion, Technical Sergeant Charles Watson of Puyallup was crew chief on a C-47 as it dropped paratroopers into France. German anti-aircraft guns fired on the C-47, but the plane completed its mission and made it back to England as one of the largest operations in human history unfolded. "The biggest thing I've ever witnessed," Watson said. "The thousands of ships, air and naval, presented an awe inspiring sight."[9]

Private First Class Douglas Scott. *Courtesy of Scott family.*

In the English Channel, a young army engineer from Puyallup named Private First Class Douglas Scott was on machine gun duty, bound to a pole at the front of a flat-bottomed landing craft by two ammunition belts. After Scott had been for enough of a ride, the captain came out to summon him back into the boat. Inside, men were either seasick or sleeping. Scott lay down on a table and joined the sleeping party.[10]

In the early hours of D-Day, Scott's 149th Amphibious Engineers approached the shoreline with a fleet of other landing crafts. Navy Machinist's Mate Third Class Ralph Bradford of Puyallup manned one of the landing crafts in an early wave into Normandy.[11] In a landing craft just a few hundred feet away from Scott's craft were two brothers and their uncle. With the sergeant's permission, one of the brothers had traded places with Scott so that he could be with his relatives.

German artillery exploded from the side of the cliffs ahead. A rocket filled with oil and shrapnel came down on the boat where Douglas Scott would have been. An inferno of diesel flames rose into the air. But then the channel was filled with men and bullets, and there was no time to reflect. "All of the sudden you're trying to get out of sight in a hurry," he said. "We swam in the water first, then we waded up to shore. They were trying to take care of some of the wounded. There was more than the medics could take care of. The tide came in and washed a few of the wounded out to sea."[12]

There were waves of metal, pounding down from the cliffs and echoing back from the American destroyers. The sound was deafening. "I didn't talk about it for years and years and years," said Al Gerstmann, who spent his youth working at the family clothing store at the corner of Pioneer and Meridian, graduated from Puyallup High School in 1942 and went to work at the Bremerton Naval Shipyard, making bolts for ship repairs. Among the ships Gerstmann restored was the USS *Nevada*, badly damaged during the Japanese attack on Pearl Harbor.

The next time Gerstmann encountered the *Nevada*, its guns were pumping shells into the German fortifications on Omaha Beach and pelting the enemy miles inland. Among the million other blasts and cries of war that day, the *Nevada*'s resounded the loudest.

Al Gerstmann's 348th Combat Engineers, stationed at Swansea, Wales, had practiced the landing for several months. It loaded into ships on June 5, but it was delayed by rough weather and stayed on board the ship until transferring into landing boats the following morning.

The first group of the 348th was almost entirely wiped out, and every one of its boats was lost. Gerstmann's group was to be in the second wave off the ship, but the loss of the initial boats required the men to improvise with smaller boats that were usually reserved for infantry. Embarking, Gerstmann's boat soon encountered a patrol boat with navy men waving flag signals to avoid the area because of a mine. Redirected toward the coastline, the boat made its way toward the landing area, which by then was so crowded with men and landing craft that there was no room to get out. The boat retreated to the ship. Soon it was dispatched to a less crowded section of Omaha Beach beneath a steep cliff north of the main landing site.

Even though the cliff offered some initial protection to Gerstmann and his fellow soldiers, they would have to make their way along the beach to the heart of the fighting, and the scene ashore was a grisly sign of what lay south along the sand. "The shore was just packed with wounded," said Gerstmann. "They were waiting to get back on the boat to go out to the hospital mothership."

Gerstmann made his way down the main landing site and took shelter near a field hospital. The hospital was far enough beneath the looming bluff that German shells just missed it. "They landed out toward the water, and everything rocked," said Gerstmann. "We were dug in there. We liked that spot to dig in, because it was all sand, and we could dig down easy."[13]

Meanwhile, Douglas Scott was scrambling around the beach dismantling landmines and other obstacles. He estimated that bullets came his way three or four times that first day.[14]

CORPORAL LEMAR CARR

Corporal Lemar Carr, a former worker at Hunt's Cannery in Puyallup and Boeing, was an army surgical technician when he went onto the beach at Normandy. "When a little squad from a Thunderbolt battalion medical section, which had gone out in a [jeep] to locate a casualty, failed to return, Cpl. Carr borrowed another [jeep] and went out to search," reported the army's *Beachhead News*.

At a certain point in the road an outpost warned Carr not to go any farther, as the road was under harassing enemy machine gun fire. But [the] corporal was determined to find his buddies. He continued on his way. The Nazis gave him a reception of hot mortar and machine gun fire.

He finally located the wounded medics, where their [jeep] had hit a mine and injured the men. He administered first aid and then turned over the [jeep] to them. One of the wounded medics was able to drive and Carr ordered them to the rear, but the corporal remained behind at the mine field. He insisted on staying and marking the field with bits of cloth and crude signs which he improvised to prevent further casualties at the same spot.

Puyallup Press, "News About Service Men," July 7, 1944; "Local Soldier Normandy Hero," July 7, 1944.

Up the coastline at Utah Beach, German fighter planes strafed the beach occasionally as members of the 101st Airborne Division made their way to the French village of Carentan. One of the men was Bob Leonard of Wisconsin, who would later come to Puyallup to work at the YMCA. Leonard was encamped with the 327th Glider Detachment in Berkshire when the command came to cross the English Channel. Leonard had volunteered as a medic's aide, earning a reputation for a strong stomach after he was the only crew member who didn't vomit on a wild glider ride to test newly invented airsickness pills.

But what Bob Leonard saw at Utah Beach late on June 6 was sickening. The glider missed its landing target and touched down some five or six hundred feet up the beach. As Leonard exited the glider, he could see on one side of the beach the yellow lines earlier invaders had left as they battled their way into France. And on the other side: "[T]he first realization I had of what war was—was a body rolling back and forth in the water."[15]

Al Gerstmann had an even closer encounter with death when he returned to his landing area north of the main beach to dig in near the rows of wounded men waiting for evacuation. But Gerstmann soon found that the beach was hard clay and rock instead of sand. "By nightfall, I didn't get a very deep hole. I got tired of digging so I stretched out in part of a hole. All of a sudden, one of the MPs was going by and hollered halt. Whoever was there didn't halt and he got shot. The guy almost fell on top of me in the foxhole. They just left him there in the foxhole, and I had company all night. He was a German prisoner of war. He died right next to me. I went to sleep anyway."[16]

Before reaching Carentan, Leonard's colonel ordered the men to dig in for the night on the beach. According to Leonard, a general appeared in the course of the digging and fired the colonel for having told his men to stay the night along the beach instead of moving into Carentan. That settled, the 327th Glider Detachment finished its march into the village, where it spent the night in the back of a church. "I was scared spitless but nothing happened."[17]

Back in the main landing zone, Douglas Scott spent that first night stretched beside a telephone pole. "Between me and them was a telephone pole," he said, adding, "I was sleeping." He continued, "The next day, trucks were coming in and out, in and out, carrying supplies."[18]

Leonard and the 101st Airborne completed the liberation of Carentan. Scott worked for the next two days on the beach, removing obstacles and landmines and evading the occasional bullet.[19]

Puyallup's Gerald Beers, Jack Wallace and George Holm came onto the beach at Normandy in the second wave. "The third day they started to bring more supplies," Scott said. "They didn't cook [well] for us the first few days. We were very hungry."[20]

Scott spent the first few days on the beach at Normandy clearing landmines and other obstacles. "When that was just about done and we were pushing ahead, our next job was to get into a little town," he said. "The only part standing there was a cross from the church, and that stuck in your mind. Every house was leveled. It was hit from the air, then from shells from our ships, and then from us. It seemed like we'd have the town in the night and mornings, and they'd get it back and then we'd get it back. That went on for quite a few days, and then we got the town."

Scott remembered the toll of battle on the men around him. Many had been killed—"I lost close friends," he said. And others were flooded with stress. "One of the young fellows from Texas, highly educated, should have been an officer, when we were in England he had nice-looking hair. When we landed after D-Day, and by the time we were past Saint Lo he was starting to turn gray. Worry. Some of them aged fast."

From Saint Lo, Scott's unit moved northwest to Cherbourg. "It was a town that really got hurt, and I remember a French lady out in the yard crying that her husband had been killed," he recalled. "There was nothing we could do."

Before reaching Paris, Scott was assigned to a new unit—so many men from his old unit had been killed or wounded that soldiers had to be reassigned.[21] Among those wounded in the days after June 6 was Private George Holm. He may have been wounded in Saint Lo. He succumbed to his wounds and died in a hospital at Vire, France. And so the two Holm brothers had been lost to the war—Johnny at Tarawa and George in France.[22]

PUYALLUP BACKS THE INVASION

Puyallup's War Loan Drive sponsored a community meeting for Monday, June 12, to promote the city's goal of $1.1 million in bonds. The meeting was organized by events coordinator Emmett Burks and chaired by Ralph Forbes. "Mr. and Mrs. Puyallup's Dollars and Cents are needed to back the invasion," read the subheading on the front page of the *Puyallup Valley Tribune* a few days later. A JAG officer described the treatment of POWs overseas, a motion picture called *Baptism of Fire* was shown and Forbes made an appeal to the audience to respond quickly.[23] The Fruitland Grange stepped up and joined the campaign for bond sales; Mrs. W.V. Young told the *Puyallup Valley Tribune*, "We wish to issue a challenge to other Granges that we can sell more bonds than any other Grange in the county or otherwise."[24] The loan drive would exceed its goal, reaching $1.2 million and resulting in a plaque on a new B-29 bomber that read, "This plane was made possible through the efforts of the City of Puyallup."[25]

Flag Day was that week. The Elks Lodge organized a parade and public ceremony. A battery division from the Washington State Guard, followed by members of local civic and fraternal groups, marched down Meridian from the Elks Lodge to Pioneer Park. The speaker for the program at Pioneer Park was Ed Eisenhower, the older brother of General Dwight Eisenhower and a well-established attorney in Tacoma.[26]

GETTING ORGANIZED

At Normandy, as the beach was secured, "Things gradually got organized," said Al Gerstmann:

We were in there to build roads out of that landing space out of the valley into the bluff up above. Eventually our group got some caterpillars and bulldozers to do the work. The group I was in seemed to be more longshore people. As the barges came in we would unload the materials off the barge onto trucks. There was also a lot of fuel and ammunition coming through— whatever Patton needed on the frontlines. I was there three months....

Eventually we moved from the lower part of the beach up the hill. There was a line of trees there where they set up some of the cooking and latrines. We dug a foxhole up there. We also had to get stuff to cover it. Because at night when they had German reconnaissance planes coming over...there was lead flying everywhere. People were getting hit in their foxholes because they didn't have covers. We finally found material to cover the foxholes. We made it big enough for two of us....

[W]e worked in 12 hour shifts. At the end of the shift I had to hoof it from the water level to the foxhole. They had a road they built to walk up there. Every day after I got off my shift, it took me longer and longer to get up that hill. The steps became closer and closer together. I got in my thinking that there was something wrong physically. I decided I was suffering from malnutrition. All we had was K and C rations. The first opportunity we had for getting more food was that the PX rations came from off the barges. Somebody accidentally dropped a case of candy, so we had candy galore for a day or two. Right away I noticed that as the caloric intake went up I did better climbing the hill. They were looking for volunteers for KP in the kitchen, so I volunteered, and after that I got plenty of food.[27]

THE GAMAUNT FAMILY AT WAR

Just after his daughter, Dororthy Gamaunt, gave birth to Leon Gamaunt III at Puyallup General Hospital on the morning of July 4, 1944, and before the measurements could be taken, her father, Norman Martin, was out at the train depot, not far from the hospital. He walked into the telegraph office and stated his purpose. The telegraph man returned a slip that included spaces for "name," "weight" and "height"—none of which Mr. Martin had. So the message to Puyallup's newest father was, "Mother and son both fine."

In the afternoon heat of the North African desert, baby Leon's namesake was sitting in the airfield barracks when the telegram arrived. Leon Gamaunt was a mechanic in the U.S. Army Air Corps. An enthusiastic messenger ran in with the news. "You have a son! It's a boy!" he shouted.

Besides Leon Gamaunt Jr. in North Africa, there were three other Gamaunt brothers in service. Roger was a pilot in the U.S. Air Corps, Johnny was a medic in the South Pacific and Julian was an infantry scout in France.

Julian crossed the English Channel to Normandy just after D-Day. When Dorothy Gamaunt thought of her brother-in-law, Julian, in later years, she

Julian Gamaunt poses with four French women after taking part in the liberation of their town in the summer of 1944. *Courtesy of Sparky Gamaunt.*

Julian Gamaunt with a woman in France. *Courtesy of Sparky Gamaunt.*

saw him in the photograph that was taken in a French town he had helped to liberate. In the photo, he is flanked by smiling French girls. In the summer of 1944, as he made his way through the fields outside the village he had helped to liberate, he was struck down by a sniper bullet between a hedgerow and a forest. He died in August in a field hospital outside Paris.

Above: Leon Gamaunt. *Courtesy of Sparky Gamaunt.*

Right: Leon Gamaunt with a soldier named Casey in North Africa. *Courtesy of Sparky Gamaunt.*

Of the surviving Gamaunt brothers, Johnny took the news of Julian's death the hardest. Johnny was the youngest, unprepared to see the sights of combat and even less prepared to accept the news of his brother's death. When he would go to get a wounded man or move a dead man, he could think only of his fallen brother.[28]

Chapter 7

LIEUTENANT VICTOR LEONARD KANDLE'S WAR

[Lieutenant Kandle] *wasn't ambitious, but he was conscientious. He did what he had to do and did it well, and his men liked him.*
—*Lieutenant John Shirley, Livermore, California, who served with Lieutenant Victor Leonard Kandle in the 15th Infantry Regiment, 1st Battalion, I Company*[1]

[Kandle] *was quite a character. He was a terrific combat person. He was most trustworthy. You'd tell him to do something and he'd do it.*
—*Colonel William Ryan, Fairfax Station, Virginia, a first lieutenant when he served with Kandle and I Company commander*[2]

Victor Leonard Kandle was born into a pioneer family in Roy, Washington, in 1921. He spent his early years around Roy and Yelm and McKenna before the family moved to Puyallup. He was an avid outdoorsman as a youth, fishing in the Puyallup River and finding every occasion he could for hiking and camping.[3]

Kandle's nephew, David, heard fishing stories about his Uncle Leonard and his father, Gene. "They went fishing, and all they took with them was a frying pan and a few spuds," said David Kandle. "Neither had licenses. The game warden didn't run them in, and he said don't catch more than you need."[4]

Essey Kinsey Faris remembered Kandle from youth group activities at Puyallup First Methodist Church. Kandle had a warm smile. He was shy at first but opened up as he got to know people. He enjoyed sharing jokes and laughs with friends, Faris recalled.[5]

During his first year out of high school, Kandle attended classes at Beutel Business College in Tacoma. Without a car, he sometimes walked eight miles from his house to class. As the possibility of American involvement in the war grew, Kandle volunteered for the army in September 1940 and began training at Fort Lewis. He was selected as field secretary to the Fort Lewis commanding general.[6]

In 1941, Kandle married Marigene Lee and was assigned to 3rd Division Headquarters in King City, California, working as a clerk. "I am beginning to like the Army more all the time," he wrote to his parents in Puyallup on May 28. "I guess the reason being that I am becoming acquainted with the non-commissioned and commissioned officers."[7]

Victor Leonard Kandle.
Courtesy of Terry Kandle.

The night before Kandle wrote home, President Franklin D. Roosevelt had addressed the nation to announce a national emergency and a military and industrial buildup.[8] "By what the President said last night, I am in doubts as to whether or not I will come back for a while," Kandle wrote. "There are rumors that we will go to Camp Ord [California] to finish our maneuvers, but you can't go by rumors, specially around here."[9]

Kandle wrote home to his parents on December 9, two days after the Pearl Harbor attack, "Just a word to let you know that I am all right. I am unable to get away from the post at present and rather expect this condition to continue for at least 3 or 4 days."[10]

It seems that Leonard Kandle didn't write home much, if at all, in the first few months of 1942. He was likely working overtime in those early days of the war. He had repeated trouble with headaches, landing him in the hospital multiple times. In early March, he decided to stay in the hospital until his headache went away.

Kandle described his relationship with his wife in glowing terms. "I believe our love is growing deeper every day," he wrote. "I dread the thought of leaving her and think I would just as soon stay in the hospital, but I guess that is not the way patriotic citizens are supposed to think."[11]

Kandle received orders to Camp Rucker, Alabama, and he departed at the end of April. Marigene joined him in Alabama.[12] She arrived in May and found a temporary job.[13] Kandle filled various staff support roles at the Camp Rucker headquarters. "I've been doing work for everyone in the building, including General Franke, General Schmidt (Asst Div Comdr), the

Anti-Tank Officer and our own office. I wrote up another speech that was given on the 4th of July."[14]

Kandle was set to become a staff sergeant in the fall but was determined to seek a commission.[15] He was in good physical shape that summer, winning first in his company on the obstacle course. And he was building a collection of books and other reference materials as he studied up for his application to officer candidate school.[16] "Anything you can send along the way of Gov. problems (pertinent), History, Geography, etc. that you can find in books, magazines or newspaper, please send."[17]

At Camp Rucker, Kandle passed a series of boards to enter officer training, as he reported in a letter home on October 10. "I would sure like to be there," he wrote to his parents back in Puyallup. "Things get pretty lonesome at times. Am glad to hear that dad is catching fish. The news about town is always welcome so send anything of interest."[18]

One of Kandle's fellow Puyallup High School graduates, Mark Porter, was an army journalist writing for *Stars and Stripes*. Some in Puyallup followed the war through Porter's articles. "I enjoyed Mark Porter's article best of all," Kandle wrote after receiving some items from his parents.[19]

With the arrival of 1943, Leonard Kandle's life changed in two big ways. First, Marigene, who was back in San Francisco by then, gave birth to a baby boy on January 2. Second, Kandle began his training to become a commissioned officer. "Am quite thrilled at being a papa & future officer (if I make it)," he wrote to his parents on January 4 after riding the bus from Camp Rucker to Fort Benning, Georgia, where he awaited assignment to an officer class.[20] After a few days of waiting, he received his assignment. He enjoyed the food at Fort Benning, and he liked his fellow officer candidates. "The fellows here are good company; full of jokes and fun," he wrote. "Notify my friends that I am now called 'Gentleman,'" he added. "We have taken chevrons and insignia off."[21]

Life was not so enjoyable the next week. "Things are getting tougher," he reported. "30 men flunked out today. So far I've got an average of 'B' in all tests. We've seen all conditions of war so far & have been placing ourselves in command of different groups." He needed a wristwatch and asked for help back home. "Send or get from Johnson Jewelers a Westlox wristwatch (approx. $3.50)," he wrote. "I'll send money."[22]

Two nights later, Kandle sat in the barracks writing home after completing a night orienteering course with his officer class with nothing but matches to light the way. "Things are certainly being thrown after us," he wrote. "You can dream how extensive this course is.…I'm sore in every muscle from exercises. You can imagine how some physically weak individuals feel. Some have already given up just on that basis."[23]

Kandle described a day in the life of an officer candidate for February 27, 1943. "Last night everyone stayed up until 12 & 2 o'clock working out a problem required in today's assignment. We had a barracks inspection this morning, for which we had to get everything ready. We got up at 6:30, put a white collar on our bunks, straightened shelves and clothes, making sure everything was buttoned, swept, cleaned rifles, ate, shaved, filled out papers to hand in on personal matters & fell out at 8:00. We then went for a short ride, had 2 hours instruction on combat orders, had a Graded Test & then moved to another area where we listened to a conference on Gasses, Chemical Warfare etc. I had an assignment in physical exercises this afternoon which I glanced at when we came in this noon. We had drill, physical exercises, Jiu Jitsu, personal inspection by a general and were finger printed tonight. Uniforms have to be changed every time the subject changes. Today's schedule was just an ordinary day's work."[24]

On March 9, Kandle wrote to his father about how he missed fishing. He also did a bit of looking forward. "When this war is over I'm going to raise me a big garden," he wrote. "I'll be in the mood to do some farming & also that may be the only way a fellow can stay alive if there is the let-down I think we'll have. The relations with Russia [don't] look very well at present."[25]

By March 9, 50 men had washed out of Kandle's officer training class, which had started with 160. With several low grades on his record, Kandle worried that he might have to leave too.[26] But he survived the next week and the next. Late in March, there was another board, and 30 of the remaining 110 officer candidates washed out, leaving less than half of the original class. Kandle and another candidate were placed in a special category—they were given a fifteen-day leave and invited to retake the course. "I feel lucky to be able to take the course over because I should know things just twice as well after I have finished," Kandle wrote to his parents. "The Colonel said he knew I had the stuff but was a little low academically."[27]

Kandle now had time on his hands but little money. He decided to hop on a military flight out of Fort Benning and see if he could make his way west. After a series of flights, Kandle boarded a train and completed the journey to San Francisco, where Marigene was working and taking care of their three-month-old baby, Terry. There he met his son for the first time. "He takes after me, especially his nose," he wrote to his parents. "His expressions are very cute. I love him now but just wait until he is a little older....He is an extremely good baby. He woke me up only once during the night."[28]

Back at Fort Benning, Kandle was assigned to what he called "the best Co. on the Post."[29] Ninety-six of the officer candidates in Kandle's company had gone through a preparatory school at Camp Wheeler. In a different section of Fort Benning from where he had been previously, Kandle raved about the base facilities, the quality of the food and the caliber of his fellow soldiers in the company. "I haven't told anyone that I have taken the course before and as a consequence I am just naturally bright in all I do while everyone who has not taken the course is always wondering what comes next," he wrote.[30] He didn't mind when he was assigned as platoon sergeant in his first week of training; he was a veteran in that role. "I'm going to like this course," he wrote home to his parents.[31]

Kandle's grades were looking good, all As and Bs in his courses, with perfect scores on grammar and geography, and he was given high marks for leadership. Then he took a math test and failed. It was a test he had passed on the first go-around. Now he was likely going to wash out again. Kandle went before a board to appeal, and a colonel on the board had little sympathy. "[H]e didn't think a man was qualified as an officer who did not know mathematics," wrote Kandle. "I guess there's no use brooding about it but it does seem like damn foolishness."[32] And so, as Kandle wrote on May 29, "The ax struck again."

Kandle was assigned to the 3rd Student Training Regiment, 6th Company, to begin Officer Candidate School a third time.[33] In the raging heat of June and July at Fort Benning (it was 113 degrees one afternoon, he reported), he persisted in his pursuit of a commission.[34] He described "running through the woods with a pack, gas mask & rifle" in the 100-degree heat of late July.[35] The good news was that he was now doing so well in his math grades that he was given the option of not attending math classes; he decided to attend anyway. "I feel confident this time," Kandle wrote to his parents.[36] He performed exceptionally in grenade and bayonet training, with an "expert" shooting score of 161 out of 175. Kandle's class set a new individual obstacle course record of 123 seconds, and Kandle wasn't far behind at 130 seconds.[37]

Kandle was put in charge of a platoon of new officer candidates, leading them through their course of studies and teaching everything from military courtesy to marching.[38] Eighty-eight officer candidates washed out on August 16, and Kandle was relieved not to be in their number. "Well guess I am going to graduate this time," Kandle wrote to his mother that day. He wrote his thanks to her for sending an update on hometown news, adding his hope that he might be stationed on the West Coast next.[39]

SECOND LIEUTENANT KANDLE

Saturday, August 28, 1943, was a great day for Second Lieutenant Victor Leonard Kandle. "The day has come & here I am wearing bars," he wrote to his parents. "We had a swell ceremony this morning. I was sad, glad & nervous. My arm is already weary from saluting so much."[40] Kandle received his next assignment: he would be a recruit trainer at Fort McClellan, Alabama, and while he wasn't looking forward to more of the southern heat, he clearly took pleasure when he signed off his letter to his parents, "Lots of Love, Lieut. Kandle" followed in parentheses by "a-hem."[41]

Kandle was thrilled to be an instructor. "I am getting a kick out of the work," Kandle wrote from Fort McClellan. "I surprise myself sometimes at my knowledge & ability to teach."[42] The army also enrolled Kandle in a pre-combat school. "Don't tell anyone but I think they want to get rid of me. Ha," Kandle quipped in a letter to his parents. "Oh well I'm learning a little bit."[43]

That fall, Marigene and nine-month-old Terry moved across the country to join Leonard in an apartment at Weatherly Hall at Fort McClellan. Kandle was glad to finally have time with his wife and son.[44]

For three weeks in October, Kandle was in the field around Fort McClellan for pre-combat training. He wrote a letter to his parents after coming into the camp from a night patrol around 10:30 p.m. "We are really out in the jungle, living in half hut, half tent affairs. We run Squad & Platoon problems every day in the [forests] here consisting of Defense, Attack, Security, night Problems & many other phases of combat." He took leadership roles several times during the exercise. "I am trying to appear not to [sic] bright & experienced in the art of leadership but am doing a fair job," he wrote.[45] He got to see Marigene and Terry once a week during this time and looked forward to being back at Weatherly Hall after field training, "unless they send me straight to combat."[46]

In November, Kandle was transferred to the 87th Division at Camp McCain, Mississippi. With a ten-day furlough, the Kandle family visited Memphis and stayed in the William Len Hotel before moving into a one-room house about fifteen miles from Camp McCain in Grenada, Mississippi.[47] "It looks as if I may see combat soon as this is supposed to be an old Division," he wrote.[48] In November, the 87th trained in the field near Nashville. "Don't worry about us going overseas for at least three months," Kandle wrote, but then he struck out "three" and replaced it with "two."[49]

Kandle celebrated Christmas with Marigene and Terry in Nashville. Then he was back in the field. He wrote a letter to his parents by firelight on the night of December 30. His hands and fingernails were "in terrible shape, not to mention my itchy dirty head," he wrote, but his quality of life was somewhat improved by his discovery of a new pair of gloves and socks in salvage.[50]

Leonard Kandle's 87th Division moved on to Fort Jackson, South Carolina, in the winter of 1943–44. The Kandle family found a little apartment not far from downtown Columbia.

Much of the company went on furlough in early February, and the Kandles had some time to settle in. "Terry walks all over the apartment now & has a good time playing with another little girl in the apartment. Of course he can't climb any stairs or open doors but he tries. Am off duty again tonight. Believe me we are taking full advantage of the short time we may be having together. No one knows how long we will be here but the policy of bringing old timers back from overseas may speed our journey. Personally I believe they have all the troops picked for the offensive. We may be sent as replacements."[51]

Kandle's battalion spent most of one week in February at a carbine range. He had the second-highest score in the battalion, with seventy-five bull's-eyes out of one hundred on both the one-hundred- and two-hundred-yard ranges. It was looking more likely that the 87th would ship out to Europe. "You have probably read in the papers where some of the boys with two or more years over-seas duty are coming back to the U.S.," he wrote home on Sunday, February 20. "Anyway there's a group going from our Division to replace them. We'll know who is going Monday."[52]

Late in February 1944, Kandle received orders to report to Fort Meade, Maryland, to join the 15th Infantry Regiment, 1st Battalion, I Company. After ten days of leave with Marigene and Terry, Kandle arrived at Fort Meade in the first week of March.[53]

ANZIO

One month later, on April 9, Kandle was on a ship bound for Italy. "I slept on deck last night & awoke this morning with the sun beating me in the face per usual.…We sighted land about 12.00 & immediately raised a pot among the officers as to the time of passing the Rock. I guessed 6.15 PM & missed it by ½ minute. I split with an officer who had 6:14 PM....Am learning a foreign language, reading & collecting a sun tan in my spare time."[54]

The 15th Infantry Regiment, 1st Battalion, I Company, landed on the beach at Anzio, Italy, in April. In the months before I Company arrived at Anzio, progress had been slow and the Allied sacrifices were costly.

Private Mark Porter's description of the preparations for Anzio appeared in the March 10 *Puyallup Valley Tribune*. "The long hours of work, the meticulous security, the stamping out of rumors was amply repaid," Porter wrote. "Jerry was caught sound asleep. The general's confidence was well founded. By early afternoon the following day, long lines of German prisoners were already filing past the regimental command post on an easily-established beachhead."[55]

But "easy" did not describe the days that followed at Anzio. "Anzio was a hellhole, to tell the truth," said Staff Sergeant Manuel Moreno of Fullerton, California. Moreno joined the 1st Battalion's H Company as a replacement, surviving on the Italian battlefront in a foxhole for three months in early 1944.[56]

The Allies were making progress when Kandle's I Company came ashore as replacements that spring. "Have been training my Platoon," Kandle wrote on May 1. "Received a pay sum (yesterday) & went to town. Spent 25c. I can get a haircut for 8 Lires or 8c & a shave for 3c but of course you are expected to give more."[57] Kandle requested American money ("It makes good souvenir material"), film, gum, candy, reading material and a collapsible heating unit. Kandle and his platoon stayed in tents near a town.[58]

Lieutenant Maurice Kendall of Melbourne, Florida, first got to know Kandle during the 15th Infantry's Italian campaign because the two officers were often being confused on account of their similar names. "I remember Lt. Kandle as a handsome young man who looked like he ought to be in college," said Kendall. "He always sort of reminded me of a frat guy."[59]

"Am still training men," Kandle wrote on May 10. "It looks as if that's all I'll do until the big push comes off. Have run into a lot of unknown boys from my old outfit. Wish I had Mark's address."[60] Kandle hoped he might contact his friend Mark Porter in Europe.

The next night, Kandle sat in a Red Cross building writing home. He explained, "[I]t is about the only place I can obtain a little relaxation. There, Italians, playing Ping Pong in the next room & then farther out in a larger room soldiers & Italian girls are dancing....I'm getting along pretty well with the talk and have gained numerous friends. No chance of hitting the front for a while. Manage to visit towns often."[61]

Kandle's letter dated two days later contained a different tone:

I got scared last night for the first time since we got over here. You ought to hear the fellows talk to-day. One fellow says he saw others go around corners so fast they filled their pockets up with dirt. I saw plenty last night that didn't have pants on or shoes either. That's the disadvantage of living in tents. They're no protection.

I got back to the tent one of the fellows said, "Did you get any fleas on you?" We know the places are lousy with them. Well, I hadn't looked but hadn't any bites so I said, "No." About that time he notices some on me. Boy, I was just crawling with them. I took my clothes off, sprayed, and bathed. I looked at my clothes after they were sprayed. There must have been hundreds of dead ones. Today I soaked them in gasoline just in case any were missed....

It was really bad last night—that was my second bad scare. The first time I heard bombs falling before they hit. They just sort of go "swoosh" going like the devil too. Before I had never heard them falling so I wasn't expecting them when they hit or wasn't wondering where they would hit. It's that that really bothers a person.

Last night I stood on the hill in front of the tent listening to see if I could hear anything. The excitement of a few minutes before had died down and lead had stopped falling like hail. All of a sudden hell broke loose again. It was so low that us fellows standing on the hill were almost directly in the line of fire. We didn't stay long. I had on my only pair of work trousers. The mud is so slick that I lit on my knees and slid on my rear going around a corner.[62]

TRAINING AND WAITING

As Kandle trained his men and waited in the camp for an assignment, many of his friends moved out to the front. Kandle's next letter was dated May 24. "Well mom & pop we're doing a pretty good job over in Italy now & I feel pleased even if I am not on the front yet," he wrote. "I believe, like quite a few others, that the war will be finished when we take Rome & that won't be long. Nearly all my friends have gone to the front. I'm still a teacher in Rept Depot (Replacement Depot). Have a 15 miler scheduled for tonight."[63]

The wait continued. Kandle finally had access to a typewriter when he wrote his next letter. "Am still a teacher," he wrote. "It's the Browning

Automatic now. Am training a Platoon to go out in the next few days to the front. Expect to be up there soon myself. I know very few officers here in the Replacement Depot now. Most of them and a good many of the troops that were here are gone because of this new push. We are really getting into condition now with at least three 15 mile hikes during the week and quite a few night hikes. Then we have at least 2 hours of physical drill a day which is quite strenuous in this hot weather we have been having."[64]

Not long after that Kandle was assigned to the 3rd Division. "Guess I'll have a chance to see Mark after all," he wrote, referring again to Mark Porter.[65] Kandle didn't waste time seeking out his hometown friend. "When I first came to this outfit I talked to several boys in the band that I knew & they told me where I could find Mark Porter," he wrote later. "Upon reporting to Bn. Hq. I found him asleep on the dirt floor & promptly awoke him. It was dark in the room at the time so he didn't recognize me at first & was very much surprised to see me, especially as a 2d Lewey."[66]

As for Private Porter, he wrote home to his parents on June 26, "Lt. Leonard Kandle is in the regiment. I've already seen him a couple of times. Always try to see him when I'm in his company looking for news."[67]

Kandle didn't write much in June on account of "our frequent moves & lack of Post offices," but he filled out American Red Cross stationery on June 26. "I made several visits of Rome....[P]rior to the fall of Rome I saw a little action."[68]

On July 13, Kandle was "putting in pretty tough hours," he wrote. "Cigarette rations just came out. I take my share but don't smoke them. Give them away or use them for bartering. The Italians will give about anything for chocolate, soap or cigarettes."[69]

"Wish I knew how long it will be before returning home," he wrote home the next week. "Things look good in the European Theatre. Am getting to miss you more all the time." He included a word to his mother, who was apparently seeking a job, about the importance of experience as preparation for work, qualifying his comments with a postscript: "The experience I am getting is of the wrong type. Sure wish I were in school now."[70] Kandle wished that he could include more information about his activities in his letters, but American troops were strictly regulated in what information they could include.[71] When he reported that he sometimes visited a certain town, the name of the town was censored. He also went swimming in "my spare time. What spare time? You have to make it here."[72]

LA FORGE

Kandle got to France in August, which is probably when he wrote to his grandparents the following: "Same old routine: Fight, move & patrol....Had my first change of clothes in one month, slept in a bed the first time in France & have had time to get better acquainted with people. When I & my sgt knocked on the door 3 women saw us as Americans & not Germans, they rushed out weeping & showering us with kisses. We found us another home. Such has happened many times....The people are swell, very polite & emotional."[73]

On the first of September, Kandle sat on the ground somewhere in southern France writing to his brother, Gene. "Well, Gene, have had my fill of combat in Italy & here in France," he wrote. "My luck holds out. I've killed several Germans, one officer & have picked up quite a few souvenirs: a pistol, typewriter, knife, car but it was left behind while we were on the move, and other insignias etc. Sold a Jerry watch for $25. Looks like we will be on the push again tonight. Have sat around for a couple of days. We have had only two killed & a few wounded from our Company which is good because we have killed & taken prisoner a good 250 Germans. I or L Company is always in the lead, K in the rear. K Company always stops if it meets anything. We are sure making progress."[74]

Kandle set the letter aside and didn't return to it for ten days. "You see what a chance we've had of mailing anything," he wrote to his brother. "Haven't shaved even for about 5 days & manage about two hours of sleep a night. Germans are running so fast that it takes a good man to keep up with them. The prisoners some pretty disgusted & ready to quit."[75]

A few days later, Kandle wrote to Gene, "We're not doing much fighting right now even though we are supposed to be surrounded. No patrols last night so I had a good [night's] sleep....We're treated with a hearty welcome wherever we go in France. If only we had time to enjoy it. We (offs) sleep in homes when we stop at a village for a while. Thought we had lost another officer last night when he & patrol failed to return. They were out all night, no radio contact, but came in this morning. All officers but me have been wounded or lost. Two offs have lost arms from Co."[76]

The next four days, what probably seemed like a much longer time, were intense. Kandle described this time in a letter to his brother, Gene: "Today is the first in a week that hasn't been spent fighting, on patrol or just plain moving. I'll give you one example of a day well spent. My platoon plus a section of LMGs were to contact K Company 6 miles away in a village. We ran into an enemy mortar & artillery barrage (observed fire) & two enemy patrols. Both parties retreated both times. I or we had a mission to accomplish. After dodging behind enemy lines, fire fights etc we finally got to town & found it occupied by Jerry & K Company in another town 3 miles away. We arrived one Lt & 3 pvts wounded & 4 shell-shock. I killed 3 Germans."[77]

Sometime after that, Kandle's company stopped in a town, and the men were put into a reserve status. On September 23, Kandle wrote to his parents, "Raining again and after having all of about 4 days without it, too. We are in a wonderful part of France now. The hills, little villages, green fields and people remind one a great deal of Switzerland. There are numerous little clear, fish-bearing streams also that catch my eye. Wish I had lots of time. I have had it pretty easy the last 4 days or so. Am living with a young couple of about 30 who wait on me hand and foot. My C.P. is in their house. Have eaten rabbit twice now and she is an expert cook. I sleep in a good bed. This will only last as long as we are in reserve. It's our first time. I give them my C & K rations in return which are just like Christmas packages to them. Of course you can imagine how tired of them we are. Am healthy yet so am O.K. I guess. Am a little more nervous than usual now but will quiet down."[78]

The terrain of France reminded Kandle of home. "The surrounding mountains & fir trees certainly look just like Washington & make me wish I were here under different circumstances," he wrote to his parents. "As it is I am not having too enjoyable of a time living outdoors all the time at this stage of the season."[79] He elaborated on this point in a letter to his brother, Gene, explaining that he was "still stomping the hills & I mean hills. The damn territory here is just like the Olympics back home & so's the weather."

It was in this letter about the landscape and the weather that Kandle snuck in a reference to a stunning combat experience two days earlier. "I killed an Artillery Major, a M.G.er & a sniper & with the help of 20 men captured the machine gun, 2 officers & 49 Germans armed with spit pistols," he wrote. "Am in for a D.S.C. & a raise but don't hold much hope. You have to lick the whole German Army & have the General pumping for you....Only one man killed since I have been Platoon Ldr."[80]

Kandle was less descriptive in his letter to his parents the day after his heroic actions: "I killed a German Major, a machine gunner & captured 2 Lts. & 49 prisoners all in one day. I had the help of my 20 men with the prisoners. You'll see the story. Mark Porter covered it. The 2^d Platoon of I Co. has been making history."[81] Indeed, Kandle's hometown friend Private First Class Porter had the scoop and described the events of that day in an article later published in the *Puyallup Valley Tribune*.

Puyallup Officer Takes Prisoners
Private First Class Mark Porter, *Puyallup Valley Tribune*,
January 11, 1945, 1, 4.

A platoon leader from the 3rd Infantry Division's 15th Regiment
did a good day's work when he and his platoon took on enemy
CP, two strong points and some stray Germans that netted them
52 prisoners and left eight dead Germans. The platoon suffered
no casualties. This division is with the Seventh Army in France.

Shortly after dawn the Third Battalion officer, Second
Lieutenant Victor L. Kandle, Puyallup, and Private First Class
Carlos Cassiano, Laredo, Texas, searched a house, looking
for a new location for their own company CP. The tenants,
collaborationists, had told them no Germans were in the vicinity
but investigation in the barn by Cassiano revealed two of them
who were taken without a fight.

A sniper was also taken without opposition an hour later a
short distance away.

Shortly before noon the officer and a patrol of five men were
interrupted during their investigation of other houses in the
area by the approach of two enemy riflemen and an officer. The
Germans fled at sight of the Americans after their officer had
first fired a burst from his machine pistol.

The riflemen and officer, a major, split up their flight,
Lieutenant Kandle shot the officer three times with his rifle
while the Kraut was running before the officer finally fell a
hundred yards away, dead. The other two men were captured by
the balance of the patrol.

On his return to the newly established CP the Puyallup officer
was sent, with 27 men and a light machine gun, to work his
way up a steep, rock, heavily forested mountain with the mission
to cut off an enemy force that was holding up the advance of
the regiment's First Battalion. On the way they contacted an
unexpected enemy strongpoint.

Lieutenant Kandle worked within 35 yards of the defenders before being discovered. The enemy put up a 15 minute fight before waving a white flag. Fifteen fell in behind the flag and three more were dead.

When a small threat developed on his flank the officer led his men around the menace and attacked it from the rear. Four were killed in the skirmish and two captured.

They had located an enemy telephone line earlier, cutting it at the time, and now followed it up to a house at the top of a hill, their original objective. One squad was sent to the left side of the house and a smaller one on the right side of the objective. The Puyallupite and the balance of the group tookup [sic] positions in front of the house.

A German came out of the house but on discovering the half-hidden Americans started to run back to the house.

Kandle had him in his rifle sights all the time and knocked him down with one bullet before he reached the house. The enemy soldier nevertheless managed to crawl into it.

Private First Class Thad W. Swiegart and Lieutenant Kandle were the first ones in the main house, the Corning soldier breaking down the door by the force of his body and the officer jumping in through a window.

Within a few minutes the platoon had 28 more men and two officers to add to their bag of prisoners.

Dark near and resistance in that sector wiped out, the hard fighting but tired, wet and cold men went back to their company area. The way was clear for the First Battalion.

"Old Lady Luck"

After his heroic actions at La Forge, Kandle was pulled from the front and assigned to a plans and training regiment. He also received his promotion to first lieutenant. "Am living in a house & eating hot chow, which is strictly rear echelon," he wrote home. "It's really a good life. Am actually living like a human again."[82]

Then he visited Paris. Kandle described his time in Paris in a letter home to his parents: "I was in Paris for 3 days rest about a week ago & it took me another 3 days or so to catch my Company. Was lucky to see Paris & so occupied during my stay that I accomplished almost nothing....Time flew so fast & I never did get everything done & then the long, cold trip back to camp & some more fighting."[83]

Kandle felt lucky to be alive. "Guess old lady luck holds with me," he wrote to his parents back in the camp. "Am getting to be an old veteran with no scars or noticeable effects as yet. Close to a dozen officers have come & gone since the France campaign started. Have had several turn-overs in personnel also. It makes it hard to train new men over again. Should be an able Lieutenant by the time I come home."[84]

October's weather was miserable, "worse than Washington could ever be these last two weeks," Kandle wrote home on October 20. "I never saw so much rain and fog in my life, and that is talking. Of course I have never had to sleep in it.—Before."[85] Even though the Allies were making progress, the weather was a source of discouragement. "It looks as if the fronts continue to move forward," Kandle wrote. "I dread this winter though with the snow, rain etc. Maybe they will issue us skiis, I hope. A Frenchman was telling me that they have a lot of snow here."[86]

A quarter inch of snow fell on November 9 and 10 and had melted by the eleventh. Kandle wasn't feeling well, and he had diarrhea.[87] With an inch of snow on the ground by November 13, Kandle wrote a letter to his parents in Puyallup. "Hey pop I'm not a drunkard but I'd sure like a bottle to knock the cold off a frosty beard on these freezing mornings," he wrote. "How about sending me one in a Cologne bottle or something similarly as strong & wrap it well. Believe it or not I'll hardly touch the stuff they have here in France."[88] Kandle was eager to get the decorations he earned. "Had word today that my two medals are in War Dept. & was told they should come back soon," Kandle wrote on November 13. "Can't be too soon. Speed may mean the difference between life & death these days."[89] One of those decorations was the Distinguished Service Cross, and as he wrote to his grandparents in Yelm, "I may possibly come home before the war is over. They tell me that a D.S.C. warrants a trip home for a while. Am not counting my chickens before hatched, however."[90]

Someday, Kandle imagined, the war would end, and he could envision settling down in Puyallup. He wanted to be a landowner in the valley.[91]

BENNWIHR

In late November, the 3rd Division captured Strasbourg. I Company incurred heavy losses during this time. At some point after Strasbourg was taken, Kandle asked Lieutenant Ryan for permission to go into the town. "I said, 'OK,'" Ryan recalled, "just get back here in time. We'll jump off at 2 [a.m., for a night patrol]. You'll have to be back by midnight." Ryan let him drive a supply jeep.

When Kandle didn't show up that night, Ryan grew concerned: "I got in the other jeep, an attack jeep, and went over to the First French Army," said Ryan. "They had him as a spy! Of course he didn't speak any French. I tried to tell them in English, 'This guy is now awaiting the Croix de Guerre,' the French equivalent of the Medal of Honor. I kept saying, 'Medale militaire! Medale militaire!' Finally they gave him back."[92]

Sometime around Thanksgiving, Kandle transferred out of his rifle platoon and into a weapons platoon. On December 6, Kandle received a huge assortment of nuts and candies from his parents, and he delved into them right away because he doubted he could take them along on his back. "I shared it with some very nice people who brought out some champagne," he wrote home. "A girl played the piano while we sang & had a good time in general. So it was a Merry Xmas." The weather was "wet and cold," he wrote. His thoughts turned homeward. "Wish I could be home but I guess I'll have to wait like the rest of the boys. It shouldn't be very long now."[93]

"Wish this thing would get over," he wrote home on December 15, thanking his parents for a care package that he received and sharing word of his new 0-3 sniper rifle. Kandle felt good about his marksmanship. "At 100 yards I can knock a bullseye out the size of the end of your thumb....Killed a German at about 900 yds a while back with an M-1, resting position, so look out now," he wrote. "They gave the 4th Platoon to me," he reported. "It's a weapons & not quite so dangerous."[94]

On December 19, he wrote that the weather was "much the same here as in the State of Washington. There is no snow but plenty of rain up until three or four days ago and lately it has been cold but nice." Before signing off, he added, "Am getting a little lonesome for home but not enough to affect my work."[95]

In the days before Christmas, the German army held on to its last remaining ground in France, an area south of Strasbourg called the Colmar Pocket. Just as they were settling in for a rest in anticipation of Christmas in Strasbourg, Kandle and I Company were ordered to join a convoy of trucks headed to Colmar. It was a damp, frigid day when the men got out to march, finally bedding down at a winery and a barn for the next two nights. Early on the morning of December 23, I Company received its orders: capture the town of Bennwihr.

I Company took its position along with four Sherman medium tanks on the edge of a vineyard. The soldiers, grouped in three platoons, followed in the tracks of the tanks through the vineyard. About half a mile along, the enemy began firing mortar and artillery rounds.[96] Lieutenant John Shirley described the scene in his memoirs:

> *Almost instantly all four tanks were hit and abandoned. The tank crews streamed out of the hatches, and several of the tanks started to burn. We moved around the tanks in a skirmish line with all of our weapons firing at German dugouts. We overran the German position on the edge of the town. My Platoon Leader was badly wounded, but we supported him, as we moved into the town.*
>
> *We found shelter in the basement of a completely destroyed house in the center of a courtyard just off the main street. Bennwihr had been destroyed by fierce fighting between the 36th Division and the Germans. There was little left but piles of rubble, and badly damaged buildings. Only one pre-war house exists in Bennwihr.[97]*

On Christmas Eve, K and L Companies entered Bennwihr to help take the area. "The days until the 29th were filled with contact and combat patrols mostly at night," according to I Company veteran T/5 Eugene "Jake" Jacobsen of Shaver Lake, California. "Any time you moved during the day they brought in 88 fire, we stayed in the cellar most of the time. All the patrols we were doing to try to make the Germans think we had a lot of men, when we were down to a precious few."[98]

Staff Sergeant George Dittoe of Peninsula, Ohio, described the "[a]wful cold weather at that time. We were outside so much, and you just can't seem to keep warm, but you get used to it."[99]

The men had missed Christmas dinner. It was finally delivered to them at Bennwihr on December 29. "When they brought it to us they told about the patrol we were going on that night," said Jacobsen, "and so there went our appetite."[100]

Lieutenant Kandle and Lieutenant Main led the eleven-man patrol that night. They moved south of town and then east along the Weiss River, where they encountered a small enemy post. They killed four Germans at the post and moved farther along the bank to take six POWs. They exchanged fire with an enemy patrol before turning back toward Bennwihr and taking five more POWs without resistance at a blown bridge south of town.

Kandle and Main regrouped in Bennwihr, this time with thirty men. Departing just before 1:30 a.m., their patrol moved south of town to the southern slope of a hill known as "Hill 216." Encountering the enemy, the Americans opened fire and killed about fifteen German soldiers. Some one hundred German reinforcements rushed in from different directions, with support from a bazooka gun and two machine guns. Lieutenant Main was hit in the leg, and another soldier, Dale Hawbaker, was wounded.[101]

Kandle ordered his patrol to withdraw its artillery and called for mortar rounds to commence. The patrol retreated back to Bennwihr.

The next day, Ryan tried to discourage Kandle from going on the mission back to Hill 216. "You're crazy," Ryan told Kandle. "You did all this stuff and you're in for the Congressional Medal of Honor—there's no question you'll get it."

Kandle insisted on going. "He was fearless," said Ryan. He knew the risks, and he was willing to accept them. He gave me a bunch of watches he'd taken off German prisoners and money and said, 'Just in case I don't come back, mail these to my wife.' He just had the feeling he wasn't going to come back."[102]

Years later, Jacobsen described the events that unfolded that night in a letter to Shirley: "I Co was down to 15 men so they pulled in 10 from K, L and from anti-tankers. We went in behind three tanks and really took a beating. The Germans were putting mortar behind the tanks and knocking us out. I got it through my head and helmet without hitting my head, two others were shot too, one in the leg and another in the back, this was the threesome who took off for the aid station."[103]

Kandle took a seat on the back of a tank beside radioman Bob Ralston of rural Georgia as they rode up the hill. Shortly after midnight, a German soldier in the darkness near the tank threw a white phosphorous grenade. It hit Lieutenant Kandle in the stomach and exploded. He fell from the tank. Ralston jumped off and saw that Kandle was dead.[104]

Mourning

Word reached Bennwihr. Jacobsen was in the hospital the morning of New Year's Eve when he learned what had happened. "I talked to some guys who lasted up there longer than me, said all the tanks were knocked out with the

Germans putting cross fire behind them. I found out some were captured, some were killed," Kandle among them, said Jacobsen. "It was right afterwards that I found out about it," said Ryan. "I was quite sad because I did my best to talk him out of doing it. I hated to send this stuff to his wife."[105]

Among American army units, the 15th Infantry Regiment had one of the highest rates of loss. Around the time Kandle was killed, his fellow army officer from Puyallup, Stuart Van Slyke, was visiting the Red Cross Officers Club in Rome, where he met up with a fellow army major in the 15th Infantry Regiment who had been a classmate in the University of Washington Reserve Officer Training Corps. Along with twelve other ROTC graduates, Van Slyke had originally been assigned to the 15th Infantry in 1940 before his orders were revoked to continue work he had underway at Fort Lewis. "My classmate told me, that of the original twelve of our class, that were assigned to the 15th Infantry, he was the only one that was still alive, and on active duty," Van Slyke wrote. "The others were either killed or discharged because of wounds received in combat."[106]

Shortly after New Year's Day 1945, Marigene and then Kandle's parents received word that Lieutenant Kandle was missing in action. Marigene wrote letter after letter to military officials trying to find out what exactly had happened to her husband. Then she received official word from the army that he had been killed in action on December 31, the date when he had originally been reported as missing in action.[107] Another letter followed from the Protestant chaplain who had officiated in the burial ceremony in Colmar.[108] He wrote that Kandle "received a service in keeping with the high principles for which he made the supreme sacrifice."[109]

"According to a fellow officer, he was leading a combat patrol against a strongly defended enemy hill position," the chaplain wrote to Marigene. "Lieutenant Kandle was riding on a tank when a phosphorus grenade hit it. He was killed by a fragment which struck him in the chest. He was an aggressive, daring leader who was well liked and respected by all officer and enlisted men of his company."[110]

Marigene wrote a letter to her mother-in-law and father-in-law in Puyallup. "You all know how dear Leonard has been to me ever since I met him, and the smartest thing I ever did was to marry him 3 years ago," she wrote. "We haven't had much time together since then—that is true, but every moment was the happiest anyone could hope for. Naturally—it is a great comfort for me to have Terry. And how glad I am that I took the baby and followed Leonard just as long as the Army would let me! At least he had the joy of living with Terry and I for a little while, anyway."[111]

There was sadness in Puyallup when people found out about the loss of Leonard Kandle. "I remember it fell rather heavily on Puyallup," said Kandle's classmate Frank Hanawalt. "Everybody was greatly sorrowed."[112]

In February, the 3rd Infantry Division and the 1st French Army captured Colmar. Then they went into Germany, across the Siegfried Line and into Nuremberg.[113]

THE MEDAL OF HONOR

When the war ended, the men of the 15th Infantry waited in Harrelson, Germany, for shipment home. In the camp at Harrelson, the army named its cinema the Kandle Theater.[114]

On June 4, at the Presidio in San Francisco, Kandle's widow, Marigene, and young son, Terry, accepted the Medal of Honor from General H.C. Pratt of the Western Defense Command. Kandle also earned the Silver Star, the Bronze Star and the French Croix de Guerre.[115]

Left: Marigene and Terry Kandle after they received Lieutenant Kandle's Medal of Honor posthumously. *Courtesy of Terry Kandle.*

Right: Lieutenant Kandle's marker at Epinal Cemetery. *Courtesy of Whitney Mullen.*

Terry Kandle speaks at the dedication of Kandle Avenue at Joint Base Lewis-McChord on August 31, 2017. *Photo by Hans Zeiger.*

Terry Kandle (*left*) and family members at the dedication of Kandle Avenue at Joint Base Lewis-McChord on August 31, 2017. *Photo by Hans Zeiger.*

Back at Colmar, it was raining when French workers dug up Kandle's body from its temporary grave for removal to the U.S. cemetery at Epinal. Phosphorous remained on the corpse, reigniting when the rain fell into the grave; Ralston and Shirley learned this when they returned to visit the people of Colmar.[116]

In recognition of his service, the U.S. Army Reserve named its armory in Tacoma for the hero of La Forge and Colmar. And in 2017, Joint Base Lewis-McChord named three of its newest roads in honor of area Medal of Honor recipients—Terry Kandle and his cousin, David Kandle, were there at the dedication ceremony to unveil the sign for Kandle Avenue.

Chapter 8

WINNING THE WAR IN EUROPE

Members of the U.S. Army Air Corps in the skies over Europe were particularly threatened by the possibility of becoming prisoners of war. When planes went down over enemy territory, it could be weeks or months before family members knew the fate of their loved one.

Air Corps radioman Technical Sergeant Barney Stemp bailed out over the North Sea when his B-17 was hit by the Germans and caught fire. He helped the other crew members to get out, and only the pilot remained on the burning aircraft when Stemp made his jump. Stemp had a serious head injury when he landed near the French coast in a potato field.

"We didn't know for six weeks where he was," said his sister, Eleanore. Stemp hid on the farm and ate raw potatoes. Somehow, eventually, he made it into the hands of the French underground. They "took him into custody and hid him and they got him back to his lines," said Eleanore. They dressed his head wound. Then they did something that Barney would recall to friends. "The French dressed him in a German officer uniform, because he didn't have to speak in uniform and nobody spoke to him unless he initiated conversation," said Eleanore. "They marched him into an area where Americans were and started screaming and hollering that he was American."

Three members of Stemp's B-24 crew survived, thanks in part to his heroic actions helping them to get out of the airplane, although they were taken as prisoners of war by the Germans. Stemp was awarded the Silver Star for his actions. But six other airmen didn't make it. Five of the men likely died in the North Sea. The pilot went down with the B-17 as he tried to fly it over England.[1]

The Battle of the Bulge

In the Battle of the Bulge that winter, two members of the Puyallup High School class of 1943 lost their lives.

Infantryman Private First Class Gordon Barker was killed in action in Belgium on January 15. Barker once worked as a ticket-taker at the Liberty Theater and helped to staff the *Puyallup Valley Tribune*, and he had written for the Puyallup High School newspaper. He was also a member of the high school debate team.[2]

Barker entered service on January 7, 1944.[3] His stepbrother, Stanley, was just seven years old when two soldiers came to his parents' doorstep on the North Hill. "They said that the President of the United States would like to thank them," he recalled. "I remember my dad going into his bedroom and laying on his bed and sobbing."[4]

The second member of the class of 1943 to be killed in the Battle of the Bulge was Barney Stemp's brother, Private Elmer Stemp, a nineteen-year-old paratrooper with the 101st Airborne Division. Elmer died on February 18 from wounds received in action weeks earlier.[5]

Elmer was good-natured with a streak of mischief. His older sister, Eleanore, called him "The Kid." She remembered him out in the family's berry field in the heat of summer one year. "Some of the kids were fooling around instead of doing work," she recalled. "'Gee, it would be great if it rained,' said Elmer. He was at the end of the row and had an audience of several people around who should have been picking instead of fooling around. He did a rain dance....Mother came out and said, 'I'll rain on you.' I never let him forget that."[6]

Elmer's classmate Virgil Harwood remembered Elmer fondly. "Having had several classes at PHS with Elmer, I was always impressed with his quiet sense of dignity and infectious friendly smile," Harwood recalled.[7]

After graduation, Stemp enlisted in the army and trained as a paratrooper and demolition specialist. "Elmer was drafted, and then he had the choice of going to different services," said Eleanore. "He wanted to go into Navy submarines, but that never flew. He picked out the paratroopers. There was always a certain amount of rivalry between Elmer and Barney. It was friendly. He was always trying to reach up to be as good at doing things as Barney. Barney went into the Air Corps and Elmer was going to top him somehow. I think being the youngest in the family gives you that kind of wish to compete, to do better than the other person did."

Army Infantry Private First Class Gordon Barker was home from training in 1944 when this family photo was taken. The former Puyallup High School debate team member and student journalist was killed in the Battle of the Bulge on January 15, 1945. *Courtesy of Stanley Barker.*

When Elmer returned to Puyallup from training at Fort Benning in late August, Eleanore recalled, "I was home from the hospital just a day or two after [giving birth to] David. He came into the bedroom, and I didn't know he was coming home. That was such a joyful meeting seeing him. He was a godfather then."

Elmer's training showed. "He was slim, trim, and mean," said Eleanore. "He was over six feet, and every inch of him was fighting man. He impressed the whole family with his looks. He had to go through dress parade, putting rifles up and down. He was sharp. One was the Queen Anne Salute. Mother couldn't take that. She didn't like the English....But he was sharp looking, I'll tell you. He was showing the defensive movements they could make to my brother Joe and my husband who is also 6 foot tall. He knocked him down. They were defenseless against them."

"When he left he was a farm boy," said Eleanore, who was among the family members who saw Elmer off on the train. "We were all standing there waving at him, and he was looking out the window waving at us. That was the last we saw him. He was going back to the east coast."[8] Elmer went overseas in November 1944.

Virgil Harwood wrote an account of Stemp's service with the 101st Airborne Division in France. The division "had lost 80% of those dropped at the Arnhem, Holland disaster a few months earlier and had often suffered horrendous casualties as the result of drops in other hostile areas, usually behind enemy lines," wrote Harwood. "Efforts at pin pointing drops were often in error as the result of unpredictable weather patterns or military miscalculation."

In early January 1945, Elmer was on guard duty on a bridge in France when he was hit in the head by a sniper's bullet from a long distance. He was taken to a military hospital, where he clung to life for more than a month. Then he died on February 18.[9]

"The day that they brought the news of Elmer's death I was at the house when the man came up to the door and delivered the telegram," said Eleanore. "My father, I thought he was going to go down on his knees, and momma"—here Eleanore paused with emotion. "My mother died in July and Elmer died in February. She just didn't want to live anymore."[10]

As Eleanore's cousin Stanley Stemp put it, Josephine was "broken hearted. Her oldest son had been shot down, then her baby died and she just couldn't live."[11] There was more sad news for the family. A few days before Stemp's memorial service at Saints Peter and Paul Church in Tacoma, news reached the Stemp family that Stemp's cousin Stewart Hamilton of Tacoma had died in service with the navy in the Pacific.[12]

A New Friend

In the march across Europe, Elmer and Stanley's cousin Eddie Stempenski, a 1941 Puyallup High School graduate and a member of the army's 83rd Division, fought on. He had survived the invasion of Normandy, the Battle of the Ardennes and the long road to Germany. He recalled the poverty of the people in Germany in the final days of the war. "One of them was so hungry that he kept reaching for food, and his friend said to him, 'Don't do that, show the Americans that we still have our dignity.' I remember that to this day," he said in later years.

Although the army cautioned soldiers against speaking with local residents, Eddie met and befriended an eight-year-old Polish boy named Lech Kabisk while he was in Winnigen, Germany. When he and a fellow soldier first saw the boy, they could tell he was hungry. So they offered him some of their rations, including a chocolate bar and crackers. With his own Polish roots and fluency in the Polish language, Eddie quickly found a friend in young Lech. Lech introduced the American soldier to his family.[13]

Then came Eddie's moment of need. He nearly lost his life when he was unable to get appropriate care for a burst appendix. "The poison went through his complete system," said his cousin Stanley. "Somehow they got him into England and had him there for four weeks trying to use penicillin, and that helped until they sent him over here to McChord. He was there for about 3 months."[14]

But Eddie always remembered the faces of the impoverished people he saw in the days after the war in Germany in the spring of 1945.

Forty-five years later, in 1990, Eddie Stempenski received a letter from Lech Kabisk, by then a middle-aged man. "It was really touching," he told a reporter, noting that Lech "remembered how we treated them, and how we fed him crackers and chocolate. And he probably had never eaten chocolate."

"There are a lot of horrible things I remember about the war," Eddie said. "But there are a lot of beautiful things I remember too."[15]

Lieutenant Eddie Myers

In the fight against Nazi Germany, Lieutenant Edward J. Myers was among the many who paid the ultimate price. To many people back in Puyallup, Eddie had been a true friend.

Myers grew up on the grounds of the Western Washington Experiment Station, where his father worked as the foreman. His mother had two daughters from a previous marriage, one who was much older and the other, Marian, who was five or six years older than Eddie. Next door to the Myerses were the Kinseys. Essey Kinsey and Eddie were the same age, so they grew up together. Since there were no boys in the Kinsey family, Essey recalled, "Eddie was like a brother."[16]

In the summers, Eddie went to YMCA camp on an island in Lake Tapps. In his first year at camp, Eddie was assigned to the same cabin with Frank Hanawalt and six others who were all slightly older. Despite Eddie's junior status, Hanawalt recalled, "He was the person that added life to our cabin. He was so funny."[17]

A few years later, Hanawalt sat in the stands at Viking Field, surrounded by his classmates and most of the town, as Eddie grabbed hold of the punt from fourth down. "I remember the determination with which he would grab that punt and tuck it away and take off."[18] Eddie was only 145 pounds, but as his teammate and friend Don Henderson recalled, "He wasn't afraid of anything. Eddie Myers was fearless."[19] As Bob Aylen recalled, "He was pretty much a born leader."[20]

The Puyallup High School class of 1940 elected Eddie its president. "Eddie was just a remarkable guy. You couldn't find a better guy than that," said his classmate Manford Hogman. "He was just a natural, I guess." Then, with a chuckle, he added, "He probably would have been president."[21]

When Manford Hogman moved with his family from Illinois to join the Puyallup class of 1940 in its sophomore year, it was Eddie, along with Ray Glaser and Glenn Todd, who made him feel welcome.[22] The class voted Eddie "Friendliest Guy" (Essey was "Friendliest Girl").[23]

Myers was a few years into his education at Washington State College when he left for the army. He began officer training in 1943, moving on

The Puyallup High School football team at Viking Field in November 1939, the year it won the Puget Sound Conference title for the third time in five years. The team had eight wins, one tie and one loss in 1939. Team captain and quarterback Eddie Myers, no. 26, stands next to Coach Al Dahlberg. *Front row, left to right*: Ralph Calligan, Ray Elliott, Ray Adams, Jack Kelley, Jack Durga, Fred Strankman and Chet Rees. *Back row, left to right*: Lind Simonsen, Francis Marcoe, Ned Jordan, Walt Parks, Buck Buchanan, Myers, Dahlberg, Wayne Snider, Gail Bruce, Bob Cochran and Walter Burr. This photo appeared in the November 21, 1939 edition of the *Tacoma Times*. *Tacoma Public Library, Richards Studio Collection, D8869-87.*

for infantry training at Fort Benning, Georgia. Eddie was a natural leader. Assigned to the 417th Infantry Regiment, 76th Division, Lieutenant Myers met up with his men at Camp McCoy, Wisconsin. He was made a rifle platoon leader.[24] Through the spring and summer and into the fall of 1944, the 417th trained for the liberation of Europe.

Lieutenant Howard Randall of Texas joined the 76th as a rifle platoon leader in August.[25] Since he was new to the platoon, he was at a disadvantage in relating to the men, but he quickly observed that Lieutenant Myers had won them over. Eddie made himself available to the GIs to assist them with personal troubles or reassure them about the stresses of war. He made camp life humane. He was a counselor and friend. Some men in the platoon were illiterate, so Eddie took time to transcribe their letters home. "He was better than the rest of us lieutenants," said Randall. "The rest of us went to town and had beers. Whenever we went into town he stayed back with his platoon."[26]

On Thanksgiving Day 1944, the 76th boarded the troop transport USAT *Brazil* out of Boston. The ship docked at Southampton a week and a half later, then the 76th marched through the New Forest to Bournemouth on the southern coast. As Christmas approached, Eddie helped illiterate soldiers write letters home and entertained them with his wit. As at Camp McCoy, there were opportunities to go out with the officers. But as Randall recalled, "Even when some local English WAAF's [Women's Auxiliary Air Force] in England put on a dance, he stayed back."[27]

Just before Christmas, the troops at Bournemouth learned that the Germans had gone back on the offensive at the Ardennes Forest on the Western Front. The 76th was ordered to meet up with General Patton's 3rd Army as it fought to keep its ground. The men would rendezvous in Luxembourg, along the border in Germany.

Christmas Day in camp was somber. The 2,500 men of the 66th Infantry Division shipped out for France on Christmas Eve aboard a Belgian cruise ship, the SS *Leopoldville*. Just a few miles from the coast of Cherbourg, a German U-boat torpedoed the *Leopoldville*, killing 802.

It was the middle of January when the 76th embarked for France. Snow was falling on Bournemouth as one hundred troop transports pushed out. The boats plied the waves at about eleven knots per hour because of the U-boat danger.

Across the channel, the 76th marched from Limesy to Luxembourg in less than two weeks through the snow, arriving in Junglinster on January 26.[28]

In the Luxembourg winter of 1945, Randall remembered, "We were all afraid that we were going to get killed or wounded in combat. After seeing the figures from Omaha Beach, we knew that it was pretty bad. We also knew that their tanks were better, and their 88-mm gun was better. [The Germans] were a veteran-trained army, most had been fighting for five or six years, and we were brand new. We hadn't been in combat at all."[29]

Starting in the early hours of February 7, several hundred men of the 76th penetrated the Siegfried Line in waves. The invasion lasted for days. The soldiers had to cross the raging Sauer River. Some were killed by German fire as they attempted to cross, and others were washed away and drowned in the rapids of the river. On the other side, the soldiers had to scale a mine-laden escarpment and fight their way through lethal German fortifications called pillboxes.[30] The area to be traversed by the 417th measured one thousand yards wide and three and a half miles long, and there were 144 pillboxes.[31] Progress was slow and deadly.[32] "A civilian observer told me afterward that he did not see how human beings could be brave enough to succeed in such an attack," General George Patton wrote in his memoirs.[33]

"On the fourth night of the big attack, K Company had crossed the treacherous Sauer River along with the rest of the Third Battalion," Randall later learned from Myers and others—Randall had been a messenger for headquarters during most of the attack on the Siegfried Line.

Casualties had been heavy during the crossing. Once on the German side, the battalion scaled the wooded slope—in many places it became a sharp cliff—and then after reaching the top the exhausted men dug in on the flat terrain of a barren tableland.

It did not take the Third Battalion long to find that the going was tough—tougher than any of the men had dreamed.

Several days and nights of hard fighting against strategically located pillboxes and determined resistance earned only a thousand yards of ground for the battalion....

The concrete and steel emplacements were mutually supporting in their firing....It was at a decidedly stagnant point in the operation that the commanders...received the order to push ahead and take their objectives.[34]

Sixteen K Company soldiers were killed, and thirty were wounded. The executive officer was killed, a captain was wounded and one of the platoon leaders suffered a mental breakdown. That meant that Lieutenant Myers was commanding officer of K Company. Under Myers's command, K Company pushed farther beyond the Siegfried Line in the last days of February.[35] He found a few moments to sit down and pen a letter home to his parents on February 18:

Dear Folks,

Just back from ten days and in the front lines. We went thru hell. Lost half the company, all but two officers. I'm acting company commander now, but hope we get a new one before long, as I don't like the job.

Will write more tomorrow just wanted to let you know I'm still OK—Lost about 30 pounds in the ten days. Going to get some well needed sleep.

Love, your son

Eddie[36]

Myers must have been grateful when his friend Lieutenant Randall came along. Randall turned over his messenger post to another officer from K Company and volunteered for service at the front. He arrived in the town where the company was recuperating after the battle. "Suddenly I spotted my buddy, Lieutenant Eddie Myers, coming out of one of the barns. I yelled and hurried over to greet him. The short, stocky officer sported a mustache which I had never seen before. He looked ten years older than twenty-two," Randall wrote.[37]

Randall spent several hours debriefing with Myers, learning the awful details of K Company's combat experience and hearing stories of incredible heroism.[38]

On March 1, "A little after noon the major called a meeting of officers," Randall wrote.

We found out that we were going to take the pleasant little town down in the valley and that we had no artillery or tank support. K Company was designated to lead the attack....

We lined up damned near in parade formation; it didn't seem as if there would be opposition. The target must have been tempting. With four-hundred men standing up and pretty closely congregated, some German 88's opened up with a shrieking, crashing salvo that shook the earth not far behind my front position. Immediately every man hit the ground and then scrambled back to his hole. Suddenly the firing stopped. Several men back toward the headquarters detachment were hurt.

The major got us out again and as soon as we were standing up the 88's let go once more.[39] [Then again. While awaiting a signal to charge forward, some men were hit. Then Randall and another officer gave the go-ahead.] *We started off the attack, running fast so that our men would be well dispersed behind us.*

Now I heard a whole mess of machine-gun fire open up from the hill far in front of us. As I ran down the barren slope, I could see clods of dirt bursting as bullets plowed into them.

Then the German mortars let go; their accuracy was amazing and deadly. One group of shells fell right into the middle of the third company behind us. I did not know it then, but that barrage got my best friend—one piece of shell fragment hit him in the stomach. If he had not eaten before the attack, he might have been saved.[40]

About that time, Randall was hit in the foot, and one of his men was hit in the backside. "I had been lying on the ground less than a minute," wrote Randall. "When I got up, the rear end of K Company was just sweeping past. Rather, they were alternately sweeping and hitting the ground as the mortar fire increased."[41]

Through the hail of fire, K Company made it into the town of Welshbillig, and some men carried the wounded Lieutenant Myers into a barn, as Randall related during a 2008 interview with the author.

"We looked down the cobbled main street—there was no one to shoot or capture," wrote Randall. "Suddenly the firing stopped. We flopped down with several other GIs beside a house. We were utterly exhausted; a mile run with plenty of push-ups thrown in had knocked the tar out of everybody. However, fortune had smiled on us—the enemy had suddenly withdrawn from the surrounding ridges."[42]

There was fighting around the town in the night, but most of the men of K Company slept wherever they could. On the morning of March 2, Randall reported to the battalion headquarters and was told to report to the aid station for his wounded leg.

"I hobbled out into the street and nearly bumped into a pal of mine from Headquarters Company," Randall wrote.

"Hi, Randy, how the hell are you? Say, did you know that your buddy, Eddie, got hit in the attack yesterday?"

"Good God!" I mumbled.

"Yeah, he got hit in the stomach; they didn't bring him in soon enough or he might have been saved. He's over here in a barn. Would you like to see him?"

"No-no. Poor guy." I turned and slowly made my way to the battalion aid station. The full impact of Eddie's death did not hit my exhausted mind; I forgot about him.[43]

The 417th and K Company went on through Germany and participated in some of the great battles of the war.

In time, Howard Randall was able to mourn his friend Eddie. When Randall stood with Bill Moyers of PBS at Eddie's grave years later, Moyers read from the stone, "Edward J. Myers, First Lieutenant, fought in 17th Infantry, 76th Division." Randall spoke up: "He's from the State of Washington, Puyallup, Washington, March 1, 1945. That was the same day I was wounded. He was behind me probably a hundred yards, maybe 200 yards, and he caught a piece of mortar fragment in the stomach, lived until that night."[44]

LIEUTENANT JACKSON GRANHOLM

U.S. Army Air Corps navigator Lieutenant Jackson Granholm took part in the war over Europe, and then he found himself in an unexpected duty assignment.

"Should I have stayed home?" Granholm asked many years later. "Flying in the United States Army Air Force was the thing to do in World War II—it was the greatest show on earth. If I hadn't gone I'd have missed my chance to earn my wings and my crushed cap, and to look like a flyboy. I wouldn't have flown all those scary missions five miles up over Nazi Germany....And I'd have missed the day the Second Air Division bombed Switzerland."[45]

After graduating from Puyallup High School in 1939, Granholm worked on a turret lathe at Boeing, and when Pearl Harbor was attacked, he volunteered for the Washington State Guard to help defend the homefront. Then, in the summer of 1942, Granholm enlisted in the army, training at Santa Ana and Eagle Field, California. He passed through the difficult navigation school at San Marcos, Texas, finally training with a B-24 crew at Blythe, California. Lieutenant Granholm and his crew were assigned to the 458th Bomb Group, stationed at Horsham St. Faith, England.[46] As a navigator, Granholm was involved with dozens of bombings of French and German targets like Evreux, Tours, Magdeburg and Minden Aqueduct.

For the airmen at Horsham St. Faith, bombing days began early. "I will never forget those rude awakenings in the British dark," wrote Granholm. "It was bad enough to contemplate a day spent flying on oxygen through the freezing stratosphere, facing death from fire, explosion, or drowning, but to be rolled, unfulfilled with blissful sleep, from a warm sack in order to do it was too much."[47]

Over Caen on June 17, 1944, Lieutenant Granholm first encountered German flak. "The sound of accurate flak aimed at your bomber is unforgettable," Granholm recalled. He also witnessed the downing of a nearby B-24 that day. "[T]he facts were made plain to me: one could die suddenly flying combat with the Eight Air Force over Europe. I'd just watched some people do it."[48]

As navigator, Granholm was constantly faced with the challenge of clouds. On July 20, 1944, the 458th changed its plans to bomb Eisenach when visibility and opportunity came together over the city of Grunberg. The American bombers leveled the city before bombing a train in the railway station. Judging from the resulting fireworks, "We had hit an ammunition train! In our blind luck, we had removed a lot of enemy war material."[49]

In August, Granholm was promoted to the office of Squadron Navigator for the 752nd Bomb Squadron and then to the rank of captain.[50]

On Christmas Eve 1944, 2,034 Allied planes from Horsham St. Faith, Attlebridge and Rackheath—the largest warplane formation ever—joined together over England for the mass bombing of Schonecken, Germany. Captain Granholm stared out the nose of his plane in amazement at "this monumental parade of destructive power," stretching at one point from the countryside of England to the coast of Belgium. Over the Ardennes forest, the Allies took on Panzer fire and lost a number of airmen. Needless to say, back at Horsham St. Faith, "Our Christmas was not the merriest in memory."[51]

The 458th Bomb Group was commended in 1945 for completing forty consecutive bombing runs without significant navigational mistakes. Meanwhile, the 392nd Bomb Group's lead pilot, Lieutenant William Sincock, and its squadron navigator, Lieutenant Theodore Balides, led nine B-24s to drop forty-eight thousand-pound bombs over what they thought was Freiburg, Germany, on March 4, 1945. Only it wasn't. The bombs fell on Zurich, Switzerland, killing five and injuring more than a dozen others. The reaction by the U.S. chain of command "was not one of instant joy," Granholm wrote.[52]

In May 1945, Lieutenants Sincock and Balides were court-martialed for their role in the bombing of Zurich. In his search for a defense attorney with navigation expertise, General Walter Peck consulted with Lieutenant Max Sokarl, an attorney, and settled on Captain Granholm as a fitting choice. "I felt somewhat like a camel among the giraffes, snowed with legal terminology, and trying to think clearly in an area in which I had no background nor training, and even less expertise," Granholm recalled.[53] Fortunately, the eccentric and charismatic Sokarl was Granholm's assistant, skillfully delivering the oral arguments. Among the jurors was Colonel James Stewart, a commanding officer from the 445th Bomb Group—but best known to millions of moviegoers as Jimmy Stewart.[54]

Granholm recalled the moment—2:15 p.m. on June 2, 1945—when the military jury reconvened to announce its verdict. When everyone was seated, Granholm glanced at Colonel Stewart. "He smiled at me. He looked human. Was there hope?" There was. Lieutenant Colonel Louis Kearney declared for the jury that Sincock and Balides were "Not Guilty."[55]

Private First Class Mark Porter

It was a Sunday morning in April when Puyallup city attorney M.F. Porter and his wife, Alma, learned that their son, Mark, had been killed in action. Private First Class Porter was the army journalist for *Stars and Stripes* and *Yank*, as well as the army's hometown news program, and had covered the exploits of his friend and fellow 15th Infantry Regiment soldier Lieutenant Victor Leonard Kandle in the fight for Europe. He had dreamed of becoming a journalist back home after the war. His life ended just short of his twenty-seventh birthday.[56]

After graduating from Puyallup High School, Mark Porter (*standing, second from left*) was a student journalist and posed for this photo with the College of Puget Sound Yearbook staff for its 1940 yearbook. *Courtesy of Mary Beaubien.*

Growing up, Mark was a quiet kid who liked to ride his bike around town, said his sister, Betty Porter Dunbar. A 1937 graduate of Puyallup High School, Mark studied journalism at the College of Puget Sound, serving as business manager for the college paper. He contributed articles off and on for Puyallup and Tacoma newspapers.

After graduating from college in 1941, he joined the army. Assigned as an army journalist in the 3rd Infantry Division, 15th Regiment, by November 1942, he covered the Allied invasion of Fedala in French Morocco.[57]

. . . .

JANUARY 24, 1943, "SOMEWHERE IN AFRICA," BETTY PORTER DUNBAR COLLECTION

Dear Moms and Dad:
Life is beautiful. It's a perfect day with clear, blue sky and warm sun. Had a shower yesterday. We just had a good dinner and I am feeling fine. All this news that Tripoli has fallen, eliminating the last shred of Mussolini's Italian empire makes everyone feel good. That still leaves Rommel and what's left of him. I heard Tunisia will be the news for a few days. The best we can hope for is the capture of Rommel. That would hurt the Germans immeasurably....

[In Africa] I may be able to save a lot of money; live a healthy life, and get plenty of mail, but I'll still be happiest when I hit American soil and have my discharge papers in my pocket. Yet, the best place in the army and the best spot overseas—yes, is right here in this particular spot, "Somewhere in Africa."

Mark

. . . .

"This job is a lot of fun, folks," Mark wrote home to his parents from the beach at Anzio, Italy, on April 17, 1944. "I get good experience from it, build up a reputation for when I return to civilian life and newspaper work and I thoroughly enjoy it. The fellows around here kid me a lot. They call me 'Scoop,' 'Ernie Pyle Porter' etc."[58]

Mark found it rewarding when a fellow soldier would come to him with a clipping of his work in their local newspaper, forwarded to them by family members. "Some kid will come up to me with a big grin and a clipping, proud as the devil at seeing his name in the home town paper. From then on he's your bosom friend."[59]

The 3rd Infantry had moved from Anzio to Naples by August, and from there, it prepared to invade France. D-Day for the 3rd Infantry Division happened at St. Tropez on August 15, 1944. "The French are almost hysterically happy at our arrival," Mark wrote home two days later.[60]

Private Mark Porter, army journalist and son of Puyallup city attorney M.F. Porter. *Courtesy of Betty Porter Dunbar.*

A more detailed description followed in a later note. "I'll never forget 'D' Day," he wrote. He described the boat trip to the beachhead and the uncertainty of conditions as they neared the landing. "A few hundred yards from the beach we met the first wave [of] boats returning," he wrote. "They had carried the assault infantrymen, the first men to set foot on the beach. The sailors gave us the high sign that everything was fine, with little or no resistance. We felt better after that." Mark also listed the gear he carried with him into France. Among the items on his uniform was a rectangular green felt patch with these words in yellow thread: "Combat Correspondent: U.S. Army."[61]

In late October 1944 in France, the skies were clear and the air was crisp as the leaves turned color and fell. Mark thought of autumn in the Northwest. "Back home football season would be in full swing, gad! How I wish I could see Sumner and Puyallup play their annual Thanksgiving game and then go home for a big dinner. Then maybe a date with Phyllis. I guess that will all have to wait for at least a year at the very least, maybe longer."[62]

He was awarded the Bronze Star that fall for "excellent work accomplished in an ardent and devoted manner. Voluntarily making trips to the front lines and spending time with the front line units, he wove into his stories a realism that would otherwise have been lacking."[63]

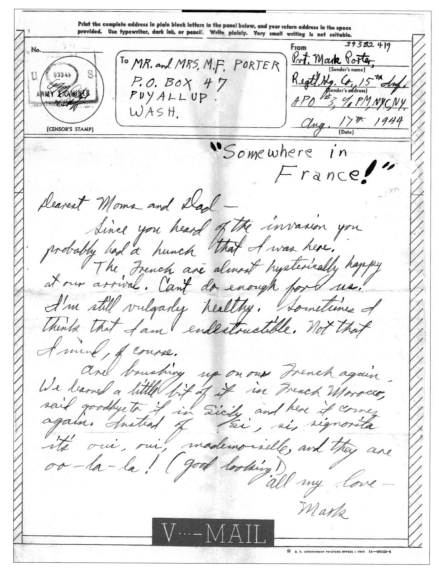

Print the complete address in plain block letters in the panel below, and your return address in the space provided. Use typewriter, dark ink, or pencil. Write plainly. Very small writing is not suitable.

No.

To MR. and MRS. M.F. PORTER
P.O. BOX 47
PUYALLUP
WASH.

(CENSOR'S STAMP)

From 39382 419
Pvt. Mark Porter,
(Sender's name)
Regtl Hg. Co., 15th Inf.
(Sender's address)
APO #3 % PM NYC NY
Aug. 17th 1944
(Date)

"Somewhere in France!"

Dearest Moma and Dad —
Since you heard of the invasion you probably had a hunch that I was here.
The French are almost hysterically happy at our arrival. Can't do enough for us. I'm still vulgarly healthy. Sometimes I thinks that I am indestructible. Not that I mind, of course.
Are brushing up on our French again. We learned a little bit of it in French Morocco, said goodbye to it in Sicily, and here it comes again. Instead of sí, sí, signorita its oui, oui, mademoiselle, and they are oo-la-la! (good looking)

all my love —
Mark

V····MAIL

☆ U. S. GOVERNMENT PRINTING OFFICE : 1943 16—28143-4

A letter home from Private Mark Porter, "Somewhere in France," August 1944. *Courtesy of Betty Porter Dunbar.*

The 3rd Infantry made its way east through Europe that fall and winter, clearing the Colmar Pocket, penetrating the Siegfried Line and ending up in the town of Nuremberg. For four days in Nuremberg, April 17–20, the 3rd Infantry fought through the town, taking ground inch by inch. The fight was intense. On the first day of the battle at Nuremberg, Mark was in a building where he could see the unfolding action, when a bomb blast rocked the building, killing Mark.[64]

"Of exemplary habits and high ideals," wrote the *Puyallup Valley Tribune*, "Mark was one of the younger generation whose future was painted in brightest colors, had not war interrupted his career....[W]hen the call to arms came, Mark was one of the first to answer."[65]

Frank Failor recalled that when Mark Porter died, "the community seemed to turn out."[66] The memorial service for Private First Class Mark Porter filled the sanctuary of First Methodist Church, where Puyallup Schools superintendent Paul Hanawalt delivered the eulogy. "Bearing One Another's Burdens" was the title of Reverend Harry Coates's memorial message.[67] Betty Porter was too preoccupied in the bearing of her mother's burden to recall much about the service. Alma Porter was devastated.[68]

Dorothy Gamaunt had known Alma Porter before Mark died and saw the change afterward. "He had been due to come home," said Dorothy. "It was just before he was coming home, and she was getting everything ready for him to come home."[69]

There had been a time, about a year before Mark died, when Alma Porter learned, probably in the newspaper, that one of her son's fellow soldiers who had been at Anzio was home on furlough in Buckley. Mrs. Porter wrote to the young man, Wilford Morford, and asked if he knew her son. On a Sunday night soon after that, Morford, all six feet, four inches of him, arrived at the Porters' doorstep. It turned out that Morford did know Mark Porter; in fact, the two soldiers were from the same company. "He left these encouraging words with the Porters," said an account in the *Puyallup Valley Tribune*: "Do not be surprised if you see Mark before many months. And don't be too disappointed if he does not come. One does not know about these things."[70]

When Mark died, Alma Porter retreated into a world of grief and never fully emerged. "Mrs. Porter, when Mark was killed, took it so hard, she wouldn't talk to anybody whose husband or son or brother came home from the war," said Gamaunt. "For the rest of her life...we'd pass her on the street and speak to her, and she wouldn't even acknowledge."[71]

But in the long days before people saw her on the street, Alma Porter avoided going out of the house at all. Barbara Martinson Jensen recalled that her father, Marty Martinson of Queen City Grocery, "was able to get to her a little bit. He would take her groceries and things. She wouldn't even want to shop. She would call, and she would say, 'I need milk, and I need

Puyallup's Gold Stars

38 REASONS WHY YOU SHOULD BUY WAR BONDS

LOCAL BOYS WHO HAVE BEEN KILLED OR ARE MISSING IN ACTION

Earl Brownlee	Vern Brouillet	Ralph Henry Keil
Howard Jaycox	Carol Lundrigan	Vernon C. Johnson
Wilbur Jolley	Wilfred Letourneau	William Hawson
Walter Lubker	Ray Glaser	Gerald O. Shuler
Doug Kelley	Bernard Pierce	John C. Morrow
Edmund Baldwin	Hugo Cloud	Ray Botsford
Howard Sullivan	Leonard Birdwell	Richard Sloat
George Holm	Donald Cyrus	Howard Thompson
Edwin Bulman	Richard Bennett	Wilmer Olsen
Jack Simmons	Gordon D. Barker	Elmer Stemp
Robert Terril	Richard Graves	Eddie Myers
Robert Bigelow	Glen Floe	Richard Hawson
Herbert Stovall	Mark Porter	

A list of Puyallup's war dead and missing in action along with a pitch to buy war bonds, 1945. *Clipping from the Betty Porter Dunbar Collection.*

this and that.' He would say OK, and he would take it to her at noon, so she wouldn't have to go out. When she recuperated, she had a great arbor, and she would respond by giving us dishfuls of grapes."[72]

THE END OF THE EUROPEAN FIGHT

The devastation of Europe was horrifying. D-Day veteran Private First Class Douglas Scott witnessed a scene that remained in his memory for decades afterward. "Going through Holland, we bombed the daylights out of it, here was some elderly lady picking up bricks and putting them back where they belong, and sweeping up the front porch, sidewalk, and even the gutter out in front of the house."[73]

In the final stage of the war in Europe, civilian and military leaders turned some of their attention to psychological warfare and humanitarian relief.

In April 1945, service clubs joined in the United National Clothing Collection for Overseas War Relief to aid needy Europeans. Drugstore owner Mel Dennis chaired the Puyallup campaign. "What can you spare that they can wear," Dennis asked the *Puyallup Valley Tribune*. Collection points were set up in the local laundry and the fire station, and arrangements were made to pick up clothes from donors. "One day soon," wrote the *Tribune*, "these people of war torn countries will be our partners in the building of a peaceful world. Will you help them now?"[74]

Lieutenant Cliff Merriott, a 1941 PHS graduate, flew B-24s with the 406th bomb squadron in the final days of the war as the U.S. Air Corps stepped up its attempts at psychological warfare:

We'd put up about twelve planes a night. Our 24s were all painted black. We went out individually and were assigned to different areas along the battlefront, France and then into Germany. Our bombs were surrender leaflets, or we went into a community before the Russians and Americans came in from opposite sides dropping messages to people to surrender. Our squadron got its load of "bombs" from the psychological warfare department.

*Oftentimes we were not too far from where the RAF was from a big site with its 1,000 pounders. To watch this from a distance was like the Fourth of July. The reason I had 41 missions was that a tour of duty in the 406*th *was 250 combat hours. It took me 41 trips to get 250 hours. At that time the formation flying in the 8*th *Air Force was 35 missions, and our "bombs" were toilet paper. Our bombardiers had to get as close to objective target as they could.*[75]

Second Lieutenant Clifford Merriott around the time of his graduation from flight school at Pecos, Texas, in May 1944. *Courtesy of Cliff Merriott.*

Merriott had just returned from a B-24 mission over Germany when he learned that the war in Europe was over. "I was one of millions who went berserk," he recalled. "I was in London on VE [Victory in Europe] plus one and that was one magnificent party. It was something else. I stood in front of the palace with fifteen thousand others and watched the queen and the girls and old Winnie come out on the balcony."[76]

Back home in Puyallup, the Methodist church opened its doors to the community as several local churches joined together for an ecumenical Victory in Europe service.[77] It was a bittersweet occasion, there at the Methodist church and in every corner of America: sadness for the losses of war, joy for the coming of peace in Europe and hope for the swift return of loved ones.

Chapter 9

THE PACIFIC, 1944–1945

Bill Hogman turned twenty years old on the ship from San Francisco to Australia in the fall of 1943. From Australia, he went into New Guinea as a replacement in the 32nd division, 128th infantry, L Company. "It was an outfit put together in Wisconsin and Michigan for their National Guards," he said. "They were the first ones into New Guinea. They were shot up so bad they needed replacements. The sergeant who I replaced had malaria. I was in charge of company runners. I had to train them in semaphore flag signals. And whenever we were out in the hills, we were right with the officers. If they needed anything, we had to send a message."

Hogman recalled his first night on New Guinea: "I had to sit guard duty with another fellow that had been there all the time. It was a little spooky. They had tin cans tied on a rope so that if you ran into it, it would jangle. There were wild pigs in the area, and [if the cans on the rope jangled] you didn't know what it was. We never had anything come in the camp at night. I guess we were just lucky."

The men of the 128th Infantry "always camped on the beaches, mostly in the coconut groves which belonged to Palmolive Soap Company," said Hogman. "It rained pretty near every day. It rained for about fifteen minutes real hard, and then it would be sunshiny again. We got good help from the natives. They carried rations, ammunition and carried out the wounded. When we needed water, the natives took bamboo three inches in diameter, knocked out the sections and rigged up a system. They even got so they could play cards with the guys."

Hogman spent about a year in New Guinea. He recalled the experience of coming under fire by the Japanese, thinking that he might die. "We were [camped] on one hillside, and the Japanese were on the other hillside and fired at the other side, every other day or so. One [shell] went over the hill. The next one came right near our hole. It did kill somebody nearby. I thought I was going to spit blood."

Then, in November 1944, his unit shipped out to Leyte. After a few weeks on the island, Hogman went on a night mission in a remote area and came under artillery fire. "We left camp about 11....We stopped at a place for some reason. One shell dropped short and got fourteen of us. I was wounded in the left arm there. It cut the nerve to my little finger. One officer, it blew his leg off and he died. I never knew what the mission was. We hiked out the next morning, and when it started getting light, we started looking for first aid. We hiked until dinnertime." Hogman found aid, but he was in bad shape.

"They flew us off the next day to another field hospital," he said. "They treated me there, but they flew us after a week to another hospital to Biak Island and they operated on my arm. The guy at the hospital said, 'If they come around and measure you for new clothes, you'll know you're going home.' So they did on Christmas day 1944." Hogman was sent back the states on the *Luraline* and spent the next year recovering in military hospitals.[1]

JAPANESE BALLOON BOMBS ON SOUTH HILL

In November 1944, the Japanese began to launch unmanned balloon bombs from the main island Honshu, and by the middle of 1945, the Japanese military had launched an estimated 9,300 balloon bombs. The balloons had a circumference of one hundred feet and a gas volume of nineteen thousand cubic feet and took about three days to arrive on the West Coast of the United States. Two balloon bombs landed south of Puyallup in the rural farm area of South Hill. The first landed, but did not explode, in a tree on Charles Massie's farm near the present-day Sunrise Development on March 1, 1945. Massie cut up the balloon and gave pieces to family members. The second bomb arrived four days later on the late morning of March 5 and exploded on George Barlow's farm off Odens Road, not far from where the Latter-day Saints church on Ninety-Fourth Avenue now stands. Joan Parks, a teen who lived nearby, saw the huge white balloon as it made landfall.

Authorities cordoned off the blast area, and curious locals were unable to access the site. Joan's brother, Orin, climbed a fence to get closer but was told to keep a distance. Soldiers from Fort Lewis came to the Barlow farm and formed a line, each man separated at arms-length as they swept the area in search of bomb fragments.[2]

PRIVATE FIRST CLASS BOBBY BIGELOW

Private First Class Robert Bigelow grew up on ten wooded acres across Fruitland from the Western Washington Experiment Station. His father was a farmer at the station. The Bigelows were a well-known family in the community. Bobby's aunt was the city's longtime treasurer and held prominent roles with the Puyallup Fair.

Bobby was a quiet boy who spent much of his childhood exploring the nearby woods and learning the local trees and flowers. He was a Boy Scout.

After high school, Bobby went off to Oregon State to study forestry. There Bobby was drafted for the army.[3] He went to Basic Training in Texas, where he formed a close friendship with a young Japanese American man named Frank Yano. They had similar personalities and interests. "My dad was very quiet too," said Roberta Yano Johnson, Frank's daughter. "Maybe that's why they got along." After boot camp, Bobby went on for cavalry training at Fort Bliss, Kansas, with the 1st Cavalry, 5th Regiment. Frank, along with his two brothers, was assigned to the segregated all–Japanese American 442nd Infantry Regiment, training at Camp Shelby in Mississippi.

Before Frank departed for service in Europe, he got married, and Bobby was the best man in his wedding.

By the summer of 1944, Frank was in Europe, where he and his two brothers in the 442nd saw some of the toughest fighting in Europe. Frank earned the Bronze Star for helping to rescue wounded comrades.[4] Bigelow was with the 1st Cavalry as they took back the Admiralty Islands and waited there for the invasion of the Philippines.

On April 28, 1944, the *Puyallup Press* carried word of Bigelow's experiences in the Pacific. "Mrs. R.E. Bigelow received word from her son, Pfc. Robert Bigelow, 5th Cav. Med. Det. that he went through the invasion of the Admiralty Islands without a scratch. He said he never hugged the good earth so tight in his life. He slept night after night in fox holes and sometimes covered with coconut logs, which kept out most anything. The

Bobby Bigelow on summer fire watch for the forest service. *Courtesy of Ruth Bigelow Jones.*

Medico boys carry carbines for protection. He will soon get a rest furlough and go to Australia."[5]

From Australia in September, Bigelow wrote home about the bonfires in his army camp, tea drinking and the local fruits.[6]

Bobby was in the fifth assault wave into the Philippines that fall. "I guess by now you have read all about us in the paper," he wrote home to his mother on November 6. "It's quite a place, we traded stuff and got chickens several times so have had fried chicken. Lots of sweet potatoes and corn too. The people here are sure glad to see us come and are a great help to us."[7] On Thanksgiving Day, as the army fought its way through the Philippines, a dinner of roast turkey and three fresh eggs was sent out to the men on the lines.[8]

From a foxhole, Bigelow wrote to his mother on December 4. The army, he said, was "doing a swell job" as it pushed its way to Manila. "Right now I've got three inches growth of whiskers and haven't washed in just about that length of time."[9]

Bigelow served at Leyte and Luzon. By the first week of February, the 1st Cavalry was in Manila. It participated in the liberation of three thousand civilian POWs at the University of Santo Tomas, where Bobby served as an evacuation hospital medic.

In combat near the Quezon Bridge over the Pasig River on February 6, Bigelow went out to aid two wounded soldiers. As he bent down to help, he was hit in the right eye by a mortar fragment. He died in an army hospital two weeks later.[10]

Bobby Bigelow at the wheel. *Courtesy of Ruth Bigelow Jones.*

Private First Class Bobby Bigelow in the Admiralty Islands. *Courtesy of Ruth Bigelow Jones.*

. . . .

LETTER TO MRS. VINA BIGELOW
Puyallup Valley Tribune, *"Letter Tells of Act of Heroism,"*
April 12, 1945, 1.

It is with deep regret and profound grief that I write of the death of your son on 20 February 1945. His loss to you and all who knew and loved him will be deeply felt in our hearts and long remembered. Robert was highly regarded by his many friends for his splendid character, cheerfulness and devotion to duty.

On 6 February our troops were fighting in the vicinity of Quezon Bridge at the Pasig River in Manila. Several of our men had made a dash through a break in the wall in an effort to cross a street which was under heavy fire. As the men reached the center of the street two of them were wounded and fell in an exposed position. Robert immediately went to their assistance and while administering first aid to them was wounded in the right eye by a mortar shell fragment. He was picked up by his comrades and given immediate medical attention and although every effort was made to save his life he died in the hospital on 20 February 1945. He has been laid to rest in the tradition of Christianity and Honor in the United States Armed Forces Cemetery No. 1, Manila, Philippine Islands.

I wish you to know that the officers and men of the Fifth Cavalry grieve with you and appreciate the keenness of your loss. Let us both hope and pray that his sacrifice will assist in making this world a better place in which to live. May God bless him and you, and give you strength to bear the loss.

F.F. Wing, Jr., Colonel
Cavalry Commanding

. . . .

LIBERATION

Among the Americans liberated at the University of Santo Tomas was Puyallup's Carl Gabrielson. Gabrielson had worked in China and Japan for American President Line prior to the war and before his transfer to Manila. Gabrielson and his wife left Japan for the Philippines just before the war, and his wife soon went back to the States. But Gabrielson was captured and confined.

Early in March, Carl's father, Axel Gabrielson, received a letter at his Puyallup home. Weighing over 150 pounds when he began his imprisonment, Gabrielson was now down to 118 pounds, he wrote.[11] And then, the same first week of March when word of Lieutenant Victor Kandle's death spread through Puyallup, some good news came over the radio airwaves about the liberation of POWs in Manila. Gabrielson's wife was in Los Angeles when she heard of the liberation.[12]

"I know how everything looked to Rip Van Winkle when he emerged from his 20 year sleep! Everyone is going around with a smile on his face here," Gabrielson wrote to his wife, adding, "We have been shut away for so long that everything is exciting to us." Released POWs were delighted that soldiers delivered plentiful food, coffee, donuts, chocolate bars, tobacco products and magazines. In a *Collier's* magazine, Gabrielson saw an ad that "showed a slice of crisp bacon, also an ad that showed a halibut steak," he wrote. "I want both when I get home."[13]

Gabrielson was home by June.[14]

PRIVATE FIRST CLASS DICK PORENTA

With the 1943 football season about to begin, Dick Porenta, at nearly six feet, five inches tall, enlisted in the Marine Corps and left home for training in San Diego on September 14. He would be missed at Viking Field, of course, but "he will be most missed in the cage sport, in which he was named all–Puget Sound conference center last year," noted the *Tacoma News Tribune*.[15] With Porenta and point leader Leonard Sawyer, nicknamed the "Dribbling Jeep," the 1943 PHS basketball team had won the Puget Sound Conference championship. Under Coach Carl Sparks, the basketball team was "as fine and gentlemanly a group of men as have ever played for any coach," said the *Puyallup Valley Tribune*.[16] The championship game would "be remembered for years wherever Viking alumni gather around to toss the bull," wrote Harold Shaw in his *Valley Tribune* column, "be it in Tunisia, Guadalcanal, yea, even in Berlin and Tokyo."[17]

As the tallest player on the basketball team, Porenta "didn't have to play much," said his stepbrother, Bob Ujick. "All he had to do was walk up to the basket and put the ball in. He probably would have [gone] to college on an athletic scholarship. He was an all-around good guy."

Porenta was also a volunteer firefighter and spent many of his nights downtown at the fire station. To make some money, he worked in the meat cutting section at the Piggly Wiggly grocery. "He was a good worker," said Bob. "Whatever he did, he did a good job."

Even with his renown as a high school athlete, Porenta was eager to join the military. Given his height, he probably could have avoided service. As Ujick recalled, "Every service turned him down, until somebody told him go to see the Marine Reserve. It was in Seattle. They took him. He went down to California to the Marine Corps base down there for his basic training, and we never saw him after that. They didn't even let him come home for a few days' visit before he went overseas."[18]

Sometime before Dick left for training, Bob asked him why he decided to go to war. "The only reason I can give is that all my friends are in the service," Dick replied. "I don't want them coming back afterwards and saying, 'Hey you shirker, why didn't you go to war?'"

Porenta was sent to the South Pacific, and he saw action at Guadalcanal (one of the destinations that happened to be listed in Harold Shaw's column about the 1943 basketball team) and Pelilu. He wrote home, but Ujick recalled that "he didn't have much to tell about, because he didn't seem like he wanted to tell about the Marines. They put those guys through a lot of rigorous training, and I don't imagine he was too happy about it. He usually wrote to my mom and she would tell us. He didn't say where they were, but he would describe the place and how bad it was or how good it was. They had palm trees and coconut trees. He did send one thing home from Pelilu. They had these little sea shells that would wash up on the shore, and the guys would go along and pick them up and make them into necklaces, and he sent one home to my mom."

"The Marines kept sending these guys to one battle after another; they hardly ever gave them a rest," said Ujick.[19]

It was while Porenta was overseas that his mother, Mary Ujick, died, early in 1945. Then, a few months later, in the Battle of Okinawa, Private Porenta was killed.[20]

Bob Ujick spent much of his life trying to find out what exactly had happened to his brother on Okinawa. He had clues but few answers. He did learn this: Private Porenta had been assigned to forward military observer duty. "They crawled through the weeds and the bushes and get as close as they can to the enemy lines, and they pinpoint all the military targets and send all that information back, and our artillery and infantry go in there and try to wipe out the Japanese." Dick stood nearly six feet, five inches tall. "How can you hide a guy that tall?" said Ujick. "But my brother did whatever they told him, and it probably cost his life."

It was Dick's Puyallup High School basketball teammate Ken Spooner who brought Dick's belongings back to the family after the war. "Ken was in some of the same battles my brother was in, but in a different outfit," said Ujick. "He was the one who brought my brother's stuff back and gave it to us, but he didn't want to talk about anything. We asked him a lot of questions, but we could see that he was a little uneasy. I imagine he could have told us a lot more than he did."[21]

WAR AT SEA

Sailors at sea took part in the horror and the monotony of war just as did the soldiers and Marines on the islands.

Warren Drotz of the Puyallup High School class of 1941 was a radar technician on the USS *Rockbridge* at Iwo Jima and Okinawa. His job entailed "looking at it, four hours on, four hours off, just staring at the scope." Drotz recalled Marines who survived the island battles coming aboard the *Rockbridge*. At Okinawa, suicide planes flew toward the ship. "There was lots of smoke around from other ships," he said. "They were mainly after the battleships."[22]

Gunner's Mate Third Class Don Henderson concluded his seventeen months at Pearl Harbor Naval Base and was assigned to a hospital ship headed for San Francisco. "It was bringing wounded guys back to the States, and we'd have to help. It took six days from Pearl Harbor to San Francisco, so we'd help the corpsmen and do what we had to do....I've seen guys with their face shot off, arms and legs shot off."[23]

Petty Officer First Class Rich Holthusen, who grew up in Fife, was aboard the USS *Nevada* when it was attacked by Japanese bombers and suicide planes on multiple occasions, particularly in the twenty-eight days *Nevada*

Left: Seaman First Class Dale Riddle. *Courtesy of Dalinda Riddle Carlson.*

Below: A dog named Snafu was a companion to Frank Hanawalt and others who served aboard the USS *George E. Davis*, DE357. *Courtesy of Bill Hanawalt.*

Seaman First Class Dale Riddle *(far right)* and fellow sailors on the USS *Major. Courtesy of Dalinda Riddle Carlson.*

was off of Okinawa. He recalled the confusion of one attack as the plane was incoming. "I was on the radio and I passed word that an enemy plane was coming in," he recalled. "The Aircraft Recognition officer said, 'No, it's a friendly plane.' The SOB started dropping bombs on the *Nevada*. I said, 'Friendly plane dropping bombs on our ship.'"

Holthusen recalled the horror of "picking up pieces of people after a suicide attack," and he saw the strange behavior of men struggling to cope in the aftermath:

> *A half hour after we were hit, one guy who was helping me to throw a body overboard dropped the bag and ran away. He wouldn't help me. One leg came out.*
>
> *There was a stretcher filled with blood during the rescue, and the guy on the other end tipped it up and got blood all over me. The guys said, "Where are you hurt?"*
>
> *When that SOB hit, I think it killed all but five Marines on the ship.... One Marine was sitting on the bitt with his arms crossed. I said, "We could use some help." He opened his arms and his guts spilled out. "I could use a little help myself." He lived.*[24]

Chapter 10

R. VERNON HILL

Behind Enemy Lines

Vernon Hill fought his war against Japan from behind enemy lines. Hill, who had worked in China as it came under assault by the Japanese in the 1930s, joined the army in the summer of 1942. "I left Puyallup that morning at 0820 on a public bus with draftees half my age," he wrote. "The draft board gave us a voucher to exchange for a ticket at the bus station. We arrived forty minutes later at the induction station located on the twelfth and thirteenth floors of the Washington Building on the corner of Pacific Avenue and Eleventh Street, Tacoma. Processing required running between the two floors for interviews, check of records, another physical exam, signing an affidavit that no changes had taken place since my physical exam three weeks before, and supplying fingerprints for the FBI....At 1545 a lieutenant standing on a chair swore all of us, 135 men, into the United States Army as privates."[1] For the next sixteen days, Hill was stationed at Fort Lewis to await assignment to basic training. Hill was sent to Camp Roberts, California, to begin basic training on September 7, completing training on December 5.[2]

Hill became an army intelligence officer, and in the war against Japan, he was sent to India on a highly classified mission in the summer of 1944. After a fifty-six-day voyage across the Pacific, Hill reported in to the Air Force Replacement Depot north of Calcutta to await his permanent duty station orders. "The daily downpour filled the swamps, which bred malaria-carrying mosquitoes to eat you alive," he recalled. "Monkeys swung in the trees. Jackals came in my tent every night looking for food."[3]

Second Lieutenant Vernon Hill, U.S. Army Infantry, and Pearl Hill posed for this June 3, 1943 photo at Griffin Studio in Puyallup. *Courtesy of Vernell Hill Doyle.*

Hill was given orders on September 21, 1944, to "AGAS, APO 627." AGAS was the Air Ground Aid Section of the Military Intelligence Service Captured Personnel and Material Branch, and APO 627 denoted the American airfield at Kunming, China.[4] He took a slow, crowded, antiquated train out of Calcutta on the Bengal-Assam Railway, "an experience I would like to forget," he wrote.[5]

He rode the train for three days and one thousand miles, arriving at Chabua on September 25. Two days later, he boarded a C-46 Commando at the Chabua Airfield. "This plane was to take me over the Himalaya Mountains, known as the Hump, to China….This was the ninety-first flight for this C-46 ferrying much needed supplies across the Hump to help Chiang Kai-shek's Free China survive the invasion by Japan that began seven years before," Hill wrote. "The planes would encounter the worst flying weather in the world over the Hump— perpetual valley mists, unpredictable air currents, solid cloud banks, drenching rains and treacherous icing conditions. Besides mountains and weather, these slow, defenseless aircraft were easy targets for enemy Zeros."[6] Between 1942 and 1945, about nine hundred aircraft were lost while flying the Hump.[7]

Hill arrived safely in Kunming, where he received ninety-eight letters— half from his wife, Pearl—that had accumulated during his travels.[8] Hill's first assignment was to take part in a rescue expedition into the Hump. Hill, another officer and an NCO were flown to an area near a Tibetan village at nine thousand feet. They delivered supplies and radio equipment to local allies, including an American missionary named J. Russell Morse. They discovered a B-29 that had crashed in the area, along with six bodies that had been buried by villagers in a common grave. Hill marked the grave with an American flag he had carried and the three Americans erected a cross on the site.[9]

Back at Kunming in the first week of November, Hill received his next orders. He was tasked with going behind enemy lines in eastern China to help downed Allied airmen make it back to safety. His was a top-secret mission, and it meant, "1. I would have no ground communications with Allied lines; 2. I would not come out until the war ended; 3. I would go alone (only American) and 4. I would not return to Kunming."[10] He spent the next few weeks assembling supplies for the journey, including radio equipment, maps and a compass; a mirror to signal planes; a bedroll; emergency rations; a Colt .45 automatic with twenty rounds; and a pocket Bible from Reverend Walter and Ellen Sadler of Puyallup First Baptist Church.[11]

After hiring a Chinese civilian radio operator named John Lam, Hill and Lam flew from Kunming to Peishiyi and then rode thirty-five miles in an army truck over dirt roads to Chungking. Hill spent eighteen days building relationships with allies in Chungking, and he hired a second Chinese civilian to serve as a field assistant.[12]

Back home, Pearl Hill began to receive returned letters with the marking "Verified Missing." Was First Lieutenant Vernon Hill missing in action? Pearl contacted various military offices and failed to receive satisfactory answers. "The sensitivity of my mission and movements were obstacles in the verification process," Hill later wrote. "It took up to two months for letters to reach Pearl, which was not reassuring when she did hear that I was all right. With that time lag it was never possible to maintain reliable communication with my family in the United States while the war lasted. Even AGAS headquarters in Kunming did not know in any given period where I was or if MIA, POW, or KIA."[13]

Hill flew into Laohokow Airfield on January 15, establishing additional connections before riding a charcoal-burning truck to Nanyang. "This would be the last automobile as well as the last road I would see until the end of the war," Hill wrote.[14] Hill and his two Chinese assistants left Nanyang on January 27 by horseback, accompanied by a Chinese military escort and two mules pulling a cart with Hill's equipment. "Rivers were crossed either by horse, rafts, stepping-stones, or wading," Hill wrote.[15] On February 8, they joined a Chinese infantry regiment on a six-day march through Japanese-occupied foothills, traveling partly at night to avoid detection and covering 111 miles in 55 and a half hours of walking.[16]

After that, Hill and his assistants were on horseback again, escorted by six Chinese soldiers and staying in villages along the way.[17] Finally, on the afternoon of February 25, Hill and his party reached their destination: a little military outpost near the village of Lihuang northeast of Hankow. "I had spent the winter getting there," Hill wrote.[18]

LIHUANG

"I set up my field headquarters in a safe house about two miles southeast of new Lihuang," Hill wrote. "It was located at the base of a narrow, deep draw in mountainous terrain with rice paddies terraced around it. There were no other structures within a half-mile. I had Chinese soldiers armed with rifles guarding the place twenty-four hours a day."[19] Hill got to work on his mission of rescuing downed airmen. "I followed a rigid schedule that kept me constantly on the move approximately sixteen hours a day, seven days a week," he wrote. "I was fully involved in security, caring for evaders, getting them out, liaison with Chinese, preparation and action [regarding] radio messages, reports, daily operations planning, financing mission, intelligence, personnel movements, evaluating Japanese military activities, collecting information for headquarters on briefing air force bases on [escape and evasion], survival, et cetera."[20]

Three downed airmen arrived at Lihuang in Hill's first week there. Each had come to Lihuang through harrowing circumstances and by means of various connections, rest stops and modes of transportation. After giving the men a place to stay, Hill wrote, "The next problem was to get them back to Allied lines." A gravel bar on the side of a river near Wu Kia Tien about thirty miles southwest of Lihuang had been identified as a prospective landing strip for rescue planes.[21]

"On 8 March I left Lihuang at 0530 with the three downed airmen for Wu Kia Tien on foot and horse with soldier escort," Hill wrote. "We have had K rations left over from my walk-in to Anhwei for lunch, as there was no place to obtain food on the mountain trail. We crossed the streams on horseback to avoid wading in icy water. At 1530 we reached the riverbed, where hundreds of [laborers] were building a runway. They were hand-carrying earth in baskets on poles over their shoulders to cover the rock base. They leveled the surface with a concrete roller pulled by a burro. The Chinese worked all night, as the first plane was expected the next day." A C-47 arrived at the landing strip at 10:00 a.m., dropped off a mailbag for Hill and took off again with the three downed airmen twenty minutes later. "It was a thrilling sight to see an American plane come to this remote area and get men out who had been shot down," Hill wrote. They called the new landing strip Valley Field and eventually extended it to 3,600 feet in length and 200 feet in width.[22]

It had been two months since Hill had last received mail, so he was grateful to get the delivery.[23] Among the letters and packages delivered by the C-47 crew was his long-overdue Christmas care package from the Puyallup VFW Post with a pack of crackers, half a pound of cheese, a pound of raisins, shoestrings, four pipe stem cleaners and seven airmail covers, one of which he used to send a thank-you note.[24] Hill reused the mailbag to carry gear along the trails in the mountains.[25]

After the Japanese captured the airfield at Laohokow, which Hill depended on for radio communications on to Chungking and Kunming, he made temporary arrangements for direct radio communication to Chungking via a powerful connection at Shenkiutsi. The fall of Laohokow and one other remaining airfield in eastern China represented the end of the 14th Air Force presence in that part of China.[26] Amid the Japanese successes in eastern China, Hill continued to rescue downed airmen. Then intelligence began to reach Hill that the Japanese were on the hunt for him.[27] On May 17, a Chinese colonel and an escort came to Hill's house bearing a document with Japanese plans to destroy Hill's outpost at Lihuang. There were plans to bribe guards and civilians, to infiltrate the rescue operation, to ambush rescue personnel using grenades and bombs and even to poison food.[28] "My operation was getting too many Allied airmen out of Japanese hands, and they were out to stop it," Hill wrote.[29]

LOUISE LYON: OSS IN ASIA

Louise Lyon, a 1930 Puyallup High School graduate, did secretarial and administrative work in the Puget Sound area throughout the 1930s before going to work at the National Housing Agency in Washington, D.C., in 1940. While in the other Washington, she took courses at Georgetown, George Washington University, American University and the University of Virginia. Lyon joined the Office of Strategic Services, the forerunner of the Central Intelligence Agency, in 1944.[30] One of the first woman OSS agents, she was assigned to service in China and Burma.

Decades later, when Louise Lyon returned to Puyallup for her mother's funeral, she reconnected with fellow Puyallup High School classmate Vernon Hill, who was by then a funeral director at Hill Funeral Home. While both had known that the other had been in the army during the war, they discovered now that both were veterans of the OSS and had served in China. In the course of their conversation, Lyon and Hill discovered "just how close they had been," wrote Larry Bargmeyer, who witnessed the conversation. "Hill was stationed on the ground in China to rescue downed Allied pilots. Lyon served in the planes that flew low over enemy territory. It was her mission to drop money, food and supplies to the military serving on the ground. When there were enough downed pilots in one place, it was Lyon's team that sent a plane into enemy held territory to rescue the pilots—and return them to Allied bases."[31]

Lyon was known throughout her life for her love of learning, independent spirit and modesty—she didn't say much about her war experiences in later years. She spent the remainder of her career assigned to U.S. embassies throughout the world.[32]

THE END OF THE WAR IN CHINA

On August 15, Vernon Hill received word on his radio that it was his duty to secure the safe release of all Allied military and civilian POWs in the Hankow region.[33] Three days later, accompanied by a radioman and an aide and carrying radio equipment, Hill set out from Lihuang and crossed over the Anhwei Mountains toward Hankow.[34] Through difficult terrain and at risk of confrontation with hostile soldiers, they made their way to the Yangtze River. Hill saw Japanese soldiers near the river, but he managed to rent a boat.[35] "On boarding the sampan I crawled under the low straw mat canopy that covered the center of the boat. The canopy would provide concealment from shore along the way," Hill wrote.[36] That night, they tied up the boat in no-man's-land a few miles from Hankow.[37]

The next day, they navigated to a known spot along the river, and Hill quickly secured a rickshaw.[38] Hill directed his rickshaw to the army headquarters in Hankow and went in to meet with the commanding general to explain his humanitarian mission on behalf of the U.S. government. Hill could tell that the general was uncomfortable with him there, but the general was gracious enough to send him in his car to a German office building. When Hill walked in, he ran into an old friend from his business days in China—Hill considered it a miracle. The man and his wife invited Hill and his assistant to stay in their apartment, at some risk.[39]

Through the Japanese general in the Hankow Army Headquarters, Hill arranged for a meeting with officers of the Japanese Sixth War Area on August 24. Hill and his civilian aide went to the meeting in a Japanese Officers' Club and sat in a circle on the matted floor with the Japanese officers. Hill explained his expectation that hostilities cease in anticipation of a formal surrender and that all prisoners of war be released without harm.[40] "Although businesslike, the confrontation was tense," Hill recalled. "The Japanese had few questions and appeared willing to accept direction on what would result in ending their eight-year war in Central China.... These representatives from the Japanese army and government gave me their verbal approval to cooperation. The atmosphere eased somewhat after snacks were brought in as we sat on the floor. As we got up, we all bowed politely."[41] For the next ten days, Hill met regularly with Japanese officials to discuss the details of the handover of POWs and other matters.[42]

Two days after the critical meeting with Japanese officials, Hill learned that thirteen U.S. Marines were positioned not far from Hankow in no-man's-land, and he went to meet them with the hope of bringing them into the city, where they could be helpful to his efforts. After running errands to get them access to the city, he found himself in the position of having to travel into Wuchang by himself that night:

> *Darkness was settling in. Chinese began to follow me en route back to the perimeter bridge....There were several hundred behind me by the time I*

got to the Japanese defense line. They expected to see the execution of an American soldier.

When I approached the bridge, I saw ten sentries on each end of the concrete structure, which was two hundred feet in length. As I stepped onto the bridge, I was immediately surrounded by six Japanese soldiers with drawn bayonets....I spoke no Japanese and saw no way to avoid an untimely end. The jabbering among the guards gave me the feeling they were bickering over who would be the first to use his weapon. Just as one thrust his bayonet to take my .45 pistol, which I still had in my holster, another miracle happened. If I had drawn my weapon I would have been full of holes.

The miracle was in a Chinese printed newspaper, the Central China Daily News, *which was given to me before leaving Hankow in the morning. I had put it in my pocket to have translated. In desperation I pulled the newspaper out of my pocket, hoping for a last minute reprieve. At that instant, in an attempt to spare my life, a courageous Chinese civilian suddenly stepped out of the crowd and approached the Japanese guards. He pleaded in Japanese for permission to translate a news item in that newspaper. It contained a story on my being the first American with authority to be in Hankow since the United States entered the war. The article gave enough description to identify me....This gave me breathing time while they pondered whether to bayonet me, shoot me, take me as a prisoner of war, or force me back off the bridge into no-man's land.*[43]

After a protracted period of indecision about what to do with Hill, the Japanese soldiers took Hill as a POW and marched him a mile and a half through darkened streets to the very headquarters where he had spent time that afternoon meeting with officials. He was released.[44]

The next day, he moved out of the apartment and set up a headquarters in an American-owned building.[45] "As soon as word got out that I was in Hankow, scores of people came to my quarters daily with urgent requests for aid of all kinds, including reclamation and protection of property, restoring utilities, first aid to the sick and wounded, protection from looters, clearing streets of war debris, fire fighting, reopening hospitals, and moving Japanese out of commandeered buildings," Hill wrote.[46]

The Japanese surrendered on September 2. The next day, ten army OSS soldiers parachuted onto the Hankow airfield. They were joined by ten more OSS soldiers on September 4, and a peaceful transition was soon underway in Central China.[47]

Chapter 11

SURVIVAL AND HOMECOMING

What became of Private Albert Tresch as a POW of the Japanese? It wasn't until August 12, 1943, that the Tresch family received a form postcard from Albert, and then another one came in September. "I am interned at H.Q. Military Prison Camp, Philippine Island No. 3; my health is excellent; I am injured and under treatment; I am improving," he indicated on the September card. And he added, "Please give my best regards to everyone." After receiving the latest communication, Mrs. Tresch told the local paper, "If Albert or any other boys interned in the Japanese prison camps would be able to tell us they would tell us to back the Third War Loan drive to the limit so that no more of our boys would have to go through what they did for lack of supplies."[1] In October 1943, Mrs. Tresch won a slogan contest sponsored by the Bruce Mercer Post of the American Legion. Her slogan was "Puyallup's Backing You." The reward was five dollars in war bonds and three cartons of cigarettes.[2]

When the Citizens State Bank put up a plaque on the side of its building downtown in June 1944 with the names of the twenty-two Puyallup men who had died in the war up to that point, the *Puyallup Valley Tribune* noted, "Albert Tresch's name does not appear as it is believed he is alive and a prisoner of war."[3]

After Tresch was in a camp in the Philippines, he spent the remainder of the war in a camp called Fukuoka I, which was relocated multiple times. At first, it was at Kumamoto from late 1942 until November 1943. Then it was moved to three different locations in Fukuoka. It was at Hakozaki just outside Fukuoka City by the summer of 1944, fewer than fifty miles from Nagasaki.[4]

Fewer than one hundred Allied POWs were held in Fukuoka I by August 1944. A shipment of mail arrived for the POWs late that summer.[5] The prisoners were tasked with building a new barracks in the camp and then with building a concrete ammunition storage facility. The prisoners were awoken each day before sunrise to be led in calisthenics by their guards before going to work.[6]

Over the long years in captivity, Albert Tresch skillfully picked up the Japanese language, and his guards took note. On one occasion, they tortured him for information by forcing bamboo pieces under his toenails and setting them on fire.[7]

Word of the war's progress made its way to Fukuoka I. In January 1945, prisoners began to hear rumors of a radio receiver that someone in camp was secretly operating. Word circulated about the Allied victories in the Pacific that winter.[8]

The winter of 1944–45 at Fukuoka was bitterly cold. The barracks had little insulation, POWs had no socks and their heavily worn boots were damp. Prisoners improvised to protect themselves from the cold, but some lost fingers and toes to frostbite and some of the sick prisoners froze to death.[9]

While many around him died in the long years of Japanese imprisonment, Albert Tresch endured.

PRISONERS AT FUKUOKA I were unloading wood from a train on April 13 when guards began yelling, "Roosevelto batai!" The men quickly figured out that President Roosevelt was dead.[10] Soon the guards brought out Japanese beer to each man. Most of the POWs drank the beer, but for them it was a moment of great sadness.[11]

One day in May, an American POW named Mr. Garcia, who was highly regarded by his fellow prisoners, began telling the men in Fukuoka I that they would go home in one hundred days. He became an evangelist for the promise of one hundred days, even telling the guards. It was a way of giving the men hope, of reminding them that freedom remained a possibility if only they would hang on.[12]

On the night of June 19, American B-29s flew over the city of Fukuoka near the camp where Al Tresch was a prisoner. A guard hurriedly ushered the POWs into an underground shelter as the B-29s began bombing the city. "Thunderous explosions drowned out the air raid sirens as the first

Daffodil Time in the Valley
Puyallup Valley Tribune, March 29, 1945, 4.

It's daffodil time in the valley again. The winds of March, unkind though they seem, have united with the sunshine of early spring to weave the "field of the cloth of gold" over bulb farms and garden until the valley is like one large flower garden.

No longer, however, is daffodil season the signal for the widespread fete of blossoms as of former years. Instead, the flowers are going to war in a big way. Not with festive dinners and pageantry but instead, the gracious blooms will go to the bedside of service men in the hospitals of the county.

It will, indeed, be a daffodil festival but with a different setting and a different purpose. The Puyallup Daffodil association is

Young Johnny Northrup hands daffodils to Pierce County Red Cross chairman Robert Lloyd. Valley daffodil growers and the Puyallup Valley Daffodil Festival partnered with the Red Cross to provide a dozen daffodils to each service member and veteran in a military hospital in Pierce County on Easter. This photo appeared on the front page of the *Tacoma News Tribune* on March 25, 1945. *Tacoma Public Library, Richards Studio Collection, D191013.*

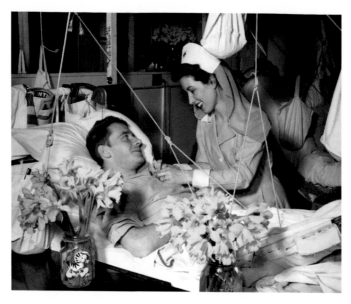

A Red Cross volunteer pins a daffodil on a wounded soldier. It is estimated that more than fifty thousand Puyallup Valley daffodils were given to service members at Madigan Hospital, McChord Field Station Hospital, American Lake Veterans' Hospital, the Orting Soldiers' Home, the Navy Infirmary and the Coast Guard Infirmary for Easter 1945, according to the *Tacoma News Tribune*, March 25, 1945. *Tacoma Public Library, Richards Studio Collection, D191162.*

answering the call of the Red Cross and acting with the growers, is gathering the lovely flowers that the soldiers and sailors in military hospitals may share their beauty. Every man will receive his gift of daffodils.

Lack of tires and gas for the past few years have made visits to the fields of Puyallup and Orting almost impossible. The Red Cross is giving the means of distribution of myriads of the golden beauties where they may well bring the message of spring—and Easter—to the sick and wounded. Symbols of the wonder of God, His peace and glory lie in the unfolding flowers.

load of bombs burst into brilliant flames," wrote Tresch's fellow prisoner Frank Lovato. "In an instant, the dark night skyline of the city burst into fiery yellow and red rolling waves of flames....Bomber after bomber made their runs, spreading an inferno on Fukuoka's factories, railroad depots, and population center."[13]

Then, one morning in July, eight American fighter planes zoomed over the camp just as the guards were calling roll. Some prisoners waved and cheered to the fighters, who responded by tipping their wings. Lovato recalled:

We behaved more like spectators at a football game than prisoners as we stood in the open yard area and blocked the bright sun out of our eyes with open hands. Flying less than a hundred feet off the ground, the planes strafed the camp headquarters, the ammo dump, and the few remaining vehicles. Anything with a Japanese rising sun was fair game to the intrepid pilots, including the Camp Work Status Board. A volley of .50-caliber bullets exploded it into a pile of splinters. The remains of the mutilated board brought some fellows to their knees and provoked peals of unbridled laughter. The status board was used by the Japanese foreman to record work progress. No matter how hard or fast we worked, we never achieved his expected level of performance, which gave the foreman justification for a more strenuous work regime. After their red and white rising sun flag, the status board was the most despised symbol of their dominance over our lives....The raid lifted our morale so much that we talked into the night like schoolboys. We retold every strafe run and roared with laughter at every mention of the status board.[14]

On August 6, aboard the USS *Orion* about five hundred yards off the northwest coast of Saipan, Stanley Stemp watched as a fleet of B-29 Superfortresses roared over the Pacific toward Japan. "We could hear and see these planes going over, big planes," he said. They had taken off from Tinian, and soon the world would know their mission. They were the planes that dropped the atomic bomb on the Japanese city of Hiroshima.

Zeiger interview with Stanley Stemp, December 14, 2008.

On August 7, the prisoners at Fukuoka I learned of the bombing of Hiroshima as men unloaded wooden slats from a railroad car. The men could detect in their guards a sense of defeat that misty, cloudy day.

Two days later, they all witnessed something they would never forget. "Suddenly, an intense flash of light lit the hazy day as though a giant flash bulb had exploded from the heavens," Frank Lovato recalled. "'What the hell was that?' asked a prisoner. We looked into the high gray clouds and searched for the source of the lightning flash that had startled us. I shrugged my shoulders and went back to carrying the wooden slats to the dock....A minute or so later a thunderous blast almost knocked us off our feet....Nobody moved for about a minute. All we could do was stare up at the high clouds over Fukuoka. This explosion was unlike anything we had ever experienced." Then the news broke over the guards' radio: Nagasaki, less than fifty miles away from Fukuoka, had been the second target of the atomic bomb.[15]

PUYALLUP REUNIONS

USS *Orion* was off Saipan on the afternoon of August 14 when Stanley Stemp received a letter from his friend George Richen. The two boys had gone through school and 4-H Club together, and both had won ribbons for the vegetables they entered in the Puyallup Fair. Stemp noticed that the letter was postmarked August 14. Richen couldn't be far away. "He sent it in the morning, and it was here in the afternoon. So I sent a letter back, next thing you know. I was on one side of Saipan, and he was on the other side. He has the signalman over there signal the beach to the ship, and he asks if I was on the ship over there," said Stemp. "He didn't realize that they just went by the ship. That's the day the war ended, August 14. You know—we went crazy. He comes aboard, he never had real fresh ice cream (he was a bloody Mariner). We're celebrating and singing and I'm walking all over the ship playing the accordion and signing until we get on the top of the deck to the paint locker. A first classman was passing out liquor mixed with grapefruit juice, and everybody is getting happier than heck, and him and I celebrated, and all we said was, 'Well, we started off together and we're going to finish up together.'"

Zeiger interview with Stanley Stemp, December 14, 2008.

The 100[16] day at Fukuoka, Mr. Garcia's appointed time for freedom, fell on August 15. Around noon that day, guards marched the prisoners back from their worksite into the camp, and word quickly circulated that the emperor had declared an end to the war.[16] "With no explanation or speech from the camp commander, the guards released us into the main yard and continued to stand facing outward along the perimeter of the grounds," wrote Lovato. "Whoops and cheers exploded from the prisoners as we realized it was actually true. The war was really over and we were still alive. Some prisoners began hugging each other while others danced, ran, and leapt with unbridled exuberance. Others collapsed to their knees and wept. One fainted and had to be revived."[17] That night, Japanese guards abandoned the camp.[18] Now the POWs had to adjust to their awaited freedom and wait for a way home.

At war's end in Fukuoka I, Albert Tresch weighed 100 pounds, a fraction of his 280 pounds when he had enlisted five years before.[19]

Four American fighters landed at an airstrip about half a mile from Fukuoka I. Several of the POWs who were out looking for food and supplies made their way toward the airstrip as fast as their weak bodies could take them. These gaunt, bearded, malnourished men wearing rags were greeted along a road by four smiling Marine Corps pilots, who seemed huge to these POWs, who had not laid eyes on healthy servicemen from their own countries in three and a half years.[20] "The approaching pilots walked proud, with the nonchalant, devil-be-damned swagger of victors," wrote Lovato. "When we met them face-to-face on that dusty road, it was too much for us to hold back our tears. Quivering, bony hands reached out to shake the smooth, strong hands of the American pilots. Handshakes gave way to hugs and sobbing. We shared camaraderie known only by men who have put their lives on the line and survived."[21] The pilots told them that help was on the way and that transport planes would soon be dropping food, clothing and medical supplies over their camp.[22]

As the former POWs of Fukuoka I waited to go home, they decorated their camp with electric lights and tents made of colorful parachutes that had been used to drop supplies. Fighter pilots returned to let them know that the navy was clearing mines out of Nagasaki Bay and that a hospital ship was on its way to the bay. It would be the American prisoners' transportation back to America. Of the forty-eight remaining prisoners at Fukuoka I at war's end, only four were Americans. Tresch, Lovato and the two others said goodbye to their fellow POWs on September 1, 1945, and walked out of the camp to find a train bound for Nagasaki. There they saw the devastation left by the atomic bomb a few weeks before.[23]

"When the train stopped at the dockside station, nobody on board moved for a brief moment," wrote Lovato. "A military band began playing 'Hail, Hail the Gang's All Here' as the doors opened." High on the mast was the American flag, waving in the blue sky.[24] Then the band played "God Bless America."[25]

> There was beauty amid the devastation, but the devastation was awful beyond comprehension. Puyallup's Del Martinson was among the thousands of American servicemen who arrived in Japan around the time Tresch and his fellow POWs were leaving. "I was at Osaka, and then I got the chance to go into Hiroshima, about 45 days after they dropped the bomb," Martinson recalled. "It was very, very discouraging. Everything was gone, leveled off, a complete disaster. Very few buildings were standing....Ten miles away from Hiroshima, the windows were blown out."[26]

HOME

Private Albert Tresch finally made it home that fall of 1945. Not long after Albert had stepped through the farmhouse door at the dairy farm on Pioneer, he asked his brother, Jim, to take him up for an airplane ride. Jim had just gotten out of the U.S. Army Air Corps, and Albert had never been in an airplane before. After years of confinement, he longed to see Puyallup from the sky. Jim and Albert drove across town to the little airfield along the river. Jim arranged to rent a plane for the afternoon, and in a few minutes, the brothers were airborne.

Jim came in low over downtown, over Pioneer Park and over Puyallup High School, and then they flew low over Pioneer Way, disturbing more than a few residents who weren't used to an airplane among the local traffic. A few dutiful citizens who were conditioned by an era of blackouts and night watches probably called the police.

But the Tresch brothers flew over their parents' dairy farm, circling above the cows as they grazed in the pasture, startling them into a trot. Near the fleeing cows was their strong old Swiss dairyman father, his fist raised to the heavens as the plane swooped up to avoid the big cedar tree in the middle of the pasture. But they were too close and the wing clipped off the top of the tree, and as the cedar boughs came in for a landing amid the cows, there was mother Tresch out on the back porch with her hands on her hips, rejoicing in the homecoming of her sons and hoping that they would come home alive for dinner. Al was thrilled.

By the time they landed at the airstrip, a fleet of police cars was waiting at the end of the runway. Out stepped the daredevil flier and his brother. Jim rolled up his sleeve to present the cops with his ruptured duck tattoo. They let him off. Obeying the speed limits, Jim and Al drove home for dinner.[27]

Chapter 12

PUYALLUP'S
GREATEST GENERATION

Late in the war, Stuart Van Slyke received orders to return home on rotation. He boarded the *Santa Paula* in Naples in March.[1] "After a very pleasant voyage, the Santa Paula arrived in New York harbor just before dusk, on Easter Sunday, April 1, 1945. It is impossible to put into words the emotions that I felt as I saw the Statue of Liberty in the harbor. Yes, the tears flowed freely from my eyes. It still seemed like a dream, I was at long last back in my own country, the United States of America."[2]

From Camp Kilmer in New Jersey, Van Slyke rode a train for four days to arrive back at Fort Lewis on the evening of April 7. "I feel as though everything was a dream. I have so looked forward to this day," his mother, Amy Van Slyke, wrote in her diary. "Stuart is home! It is so wonderful. The train was over an hour late but finally came creeping in. There were so many soldiers getting off that it was several moments before we saw Stuart. He is so brown and looks strange with a mustache, but looks wonderfully well."[3]

It had been more than three years since Stuart Van Slyke was home. He wrote:

> *On the way home to Puyallup it rained cats and dogs, in typical Washington weather. Now I felt at home. It was raining…On the way home, we stopped to see my grandparents. They were surprised and delighted to see me. Mother apparently did not tell them we would stop on our way home. We only stayed a few minutes and then we left for our home. It was quite a*

Seaman First Class Dale Riddle was home in North Puyallup when he posed next to this car. *Courtesy of Dalinda Riddle Carlson.*

thrill when we drove into the driveway of our home. To me, it looked just as I remembered it. When I got inside, I immediately noticed that the inside of the house was freshly painted and papered. My bedroom was all fixed up. Mother and father had done everything possible to make things pleasant for me and to make me feel at home. Boy, I was home again. Father had a nice fire in the fireplace and we had a cup of hot tea and cinnamon toast as we talked, before going to bed.[4]

Van Slyke checked in at Fort Lewis the next morning and was back home that afternoon. "It seemed that all our friends and neighbors stopped by to chat," he wrote.[5] Van Slyke went on dates with women he hadn't seen for years.[6] It was a process of catching up with life at home and reflecting on what had happened in faraway places. One Saturday, Stuart went shopping with his mother in downtown Puyallup, and then his father joined them for lunch. "Stuart hurried home to meet the wife of one of the men of his squadron who was killed in Africa," Amy Van Slyke wrote for April 21. "After they left, he and I lay on the couch for an hour and listened to a symphony program. I think it was the most delightful hour we have spent since he came home."[7]

Family members had their own processing to do. The men who came home were different than when they left for war. "Tonight, we all had dinner at the Clements [neighbors from across the street]. Fred and Helen [Hoyt] were there too," Amy Van Slyke wrote in her diary for Thursday, April 26. "I think Stuart enjoyed dinner. He is growing very irritable and I think he is anxious to get away. I am so bewildered but I know we are warned that our boys will be different. I suppose one trouble is they go away boys and come home men. The first week he seemed so happy to be

Hal Schimling, 1935 Puyallup High School alum, was a catcher for the Tacoma Tigers baseball team before the war. He served in the army's 41st Medic Corps in the South Pacific for three years. Just off of active duty when this photo was taken for the June 20, 1945 edition of the *Tacoma Times*, Schimling headed east to play for the St. Louis Browns. He later served in the Tacoma Police Department. *Tacoma Public Library, Richards Studio Collection, D-19698-1, TPL-8673.*

home. Now it seems as though everything we do irritates him. I can't bear to think of his going. I thought I wouldn't mind it so much when he was to be in this country but I can hardly think about it without crying."[8]

MOURNING THE LOSS

Unanswered questions remained at war's end. What became of those men with the status of MIA, such as the case of twenty-seven-year-old U.S. Army Air Corps major Dick Graves, who was reported missing in action over Dulsberg, Germany, on February 23, 1945? Dick graduated from Puyallup High School in 1935 and from Washington State College in 1939, joined the air corps in 1940 and was an instructor at Randolph Field and Kelley Field. He married Mary Kallenberger in August 1942, and they had a son named Richard Jr. In 1944, Graves was sent to England to command the 413th Fighter Squadron of the 9th Air Force. It was not until October that Dick's mother get word at her home on River Road that he was presumed to have been killed in action. "He would have been 28 October 13," said the report in the *Puyallup Valley Tribune*.[9]

The very date that Graves went missing, February 23, 1945, so did Staff Sergeant Kendric Johnson of the air corps, who vanished in the Pacific when a C-47 Skytrain transport carrying twenty men was lost at sea. It was thought to have gone down in a storm, but time passed and no official word arrived about what had happened. Then, late in March 1946, more than a year later, word came to Staff Sergeant Johnson's mother on Seventh Avenue Northwest that he had been killed in service. A Puyallup High School alum, Johnson had enlisted on December 8, 1941, and left for service in the Pacific in May 1944. He served at New Guinea, Leyte and Netherland, East Indies.[10]

For those who had experienced loss in the war, the process of mourning went on long after the war was over. Elmer Stemp was buried in France, but his family decided to have him reburied at Woodbine Cemetery in Puyallup in 1948. Elmer's casket came in on a train at Union Station in Tacoma. "My dad and husband and I went down to Union Station when they brought the caskets in," said Elmer's sister, Eleanore Stemp Brecht, whose mother had died shortly after Elmer, apparently of a broken heart. "My poor dad, when he saw that casket, he said, 'If I could just look inside.' He was going through that last day all over again."[11]

JAPANESE AMERICANS AFTER THE WAR

Japanese Americans who had survived the internment moved on and tried to rebuild their lives.

Yoshiko Yamaji Nogaki, a 1938 PHS graduate, moved to Seattle. She cherished fond memories of her family's berry farming and her years at Puyallup High School. "I like to remember the beautiful valley that it was," she said. "Then the evacuation came. I have been back there, but it does not bring back good memories. It's not the Puyallup I knew."[12]

Kazuo Yamane, Art Yamada and Tom Takemura of the Puyallup Valley Japanese-American Citizens' League worked with Senator Harry Cain and Representative Thor Tollefson to secure reparations for Japanese Americans who had been interned. In the state legislature, Representatives Frank "Buster" Brouillet and Len Sawyer led the fight to repeal a provision in the state constitution that prevented non-citizen aliens from owning land. The measure twice failed as a ballot referendum. Then, with Takemura's organizing skill on the third round, the repeal was passed.[13]

The Nakamura family returned to Fife after the war. Kaz Nakamura (*standing at left*) became a regional leader in the construction industry. *Courtesy of Kim Nakamura.*

Stogie Kawabata, Victor "Junks" Ikeda, Sean Ohashi, Fred Orton, Mary Abo, Cho Shimizu and Elsie Taniguchi pose in a replica of a Camp Harmony housing unit at the Washington State Fair seventy-five years after the internment of Japanese Americans in the fairgrounds. *Courtesy of Elsie Yotsuuye Taniguchi, Puyallup Valley Chapter, Japanese American Citizens League.*

Although many Puyallup Valley Japanese Americans moved elsewhere after the war, Bob and Frank Mizukami returned to their *furusato*—their home—to give even more to the community that they and their fallen brother, William, left in 1942. Bob and Frank resumed their father's greenhouse business in Fife. After helping to incorporate the city of Fife in February 1957, Bob sat on the city council, serving as mayor from 1980 to 1987. "I was proud to become mayor of my native area that I was evacuated from, booted out, so to speak," he said.

Mizukami once visited Puyallup High School to talk about how his life changed in May 1942, two years after his graduation from Fife High School and several months after the beginning of World War II. He told about the evacuation orders, about leaving behind his home and his family's greenhouse business, about entering the Puyallup fairgrounds, about the barracks and the barbed wire and the year that there was no fair and, ultimately, about the prejudice. "Most students from Puyallup High School didn't know anything about those things," he said. "They were surprised to hear that such a thing would be happening in our country, in our own backyard."[14]

For the seventy-fifth anniversary of Camp Harmony during the fair in 2017, hundreds of Camp Harmony survivors and their friends joined together in a remembrance event at the fairgrounds Coca-Cola Stage. For some survivors, advanced in age, it was their first time back in the fairgrounds since they departed for Minidoka in 1942.

MOVING ON, SERVING

The men and women of Puyallup's World War II generation went on with their lives. They focused on the families, their careers and their community. Some went on to other places in the country, and many came home to Puyallup.

After some years working in Washington, D.C., after the war, Vernon Hill came home to Puyallup to run his family's funeral home, serve as president of the Kiwanis Club and the American Legion and write his memoirs. "He was a quiet gentleman," wrote his daughter, Vernell Hill Doyle. "The key to my father's successful and happy life was that he spent his whole life devoting it to other people."[15]

In the years after the war, veterans from other parts of the country made Puyallup their home. D-Day veteran Bob Leonard came to Puyallup in the

The Veterans of Foreign Wars entered this float in Puyallup's March 30, 1946 Daffodil Parade, the first such parade in years. On the float, Lady Liberty stands over uniformed service members and a large globe. This photo appeared on the front page of the March 31, 1946 *Tacoma News Tribune*. *Tacoma Public Library, Richards Studio Collection, D-21802-22, TPL-8695.*

1950s to run the YMCA. There was John Cooper, who had been a POW of the Germans, and Ed Saylor, one of the last surviving Doolittle Raiders. Roald Halmo, one of Leonard Kandle's fellow soldiers from the 3rd Divison, 15th Infantry, I Company, moved to Puyallup after the war.[16] And Master Sergeant Llewellyn Chilson of the army, recipient of three Distinguished Service Crosses after service in North Africa and Europe, moved to Puyallup after retiring from the service.

Some were able to talk about their war experiences. Others said little. Roy Mitchell from the PHS class of 1941 was wounded in action at the Battle of the Bulge, but his friend Bob Aylen said, "He never talked much about it." Aylen and Mitchell purchased bricks at the Puyallup Veterans Memorial next to each other.[17]

Elmer Stemp's cousin Barney Stemp, who bailed out of his B-17 over the North Sea, went on to become a prominent music educator in central

California. But as his cousin Eleanore Stemp Brecht said, "He wasn't the same person when he came back. He was like a lovable rascal in high school. Jumping out at 20,000 feet never left him. When he left from SeaTac, I never saw anybody more reluctant to do that in a prop plane after the war." When Stemp died in 1980, the air force scattered his ashes over the North Sea, as he had requested.[18]

REFLECTING ON THE WAR

Veterans looked back on their war service and had years to reflect on the dramatic experiences they lived through. "Sometimes you can close your eyes and you can still see things that you'd done. I think when you're in a situation like that there you do what comes first and you don't worry about the consequences," D-Day veteran Douglas Scott told the author in a 2008 interview.

Service members walked alongside the car carrying Governor Mon Wallgren in the 1946 Daffodil Parade. About thirty thousand spectators turned out for the ninety-minute-long parade through the streets of Puyallup. This photo appeared on the front page of the March 31, 1946 *Tacoma News Tribune. Tacoma Public Library, Richards Studio Collection, D21802-8.*

A view of the first postwar Daffodil Parade down the Meridian, March 30, 1946. *Tacoma Public Library, Richards Studio Collection, D21802-31.*

Most World War II veterans looked back on their service with humility, happy to share credit and acknowledge the combined contributions of their entire generation. "I always figured the war was something like a co-op," said Bill Hogman, who nearly lost his life in a shell blast at Leyte. "We go to war, and the folks at home go to work at the airplane plant and munition plant. I was never sorry that I went in or got hurt or anything. I was just glad to do what could be done." Hogman's brother, Manford, tried to enlist, but he was medically disqualified for a case of tuberculosis. "I didn't get to go in the service. But I wanted to go real bad," he said.[19]

RECONNECTING

Some veterans tried to reconnect with old buddies years later. By the early 1990s, Bill Hogman was eager to reconnect with a wartime friend with whom he'd lost touch. Hogman drove to Tennessee in 1992 in search of Billy Spight, his radio man in the 32nd Division, 128th infantry, Company L. It was Billy who was with Bill on the night he was wounded in a shell blast at Leyte and who took over his duties in the battle for the Philippines after Bill was sent back to the States on a hospital ship. Hogman had no luck finding Spight, so he tried again in 1996. This time, it worked. Hogman and his wife drove across country and spent five days with Spight.

A year and a half after the reunion, Billy Spight passed away. "I knew he had gotten leukemia, and I wanted to go back to see him again," said Hogman. "The family said they didn't want me to come and see him as he was. A couple days before he died, he got his uniform on and polished up the buttons. I wished at times I had gone back for the funeral. You get so close to those guys during war that you really miss them. I still think about him quite often."

In 1999, Hogman traveled back to New Guinea to visit his company clerk, who had taken up residence on the Pacific island after the war.[20]

Veterans who lost friends in the war made efforts to connect with the families of the fallen. Bobby Bigelow's friend Frank Yano became a postal carrier, but he said little about the war. "It was hard for him to talk about Bobby," said Roberta Yano Johnson, whose parents named her after Bobby, but she picked up pieces of the story over time. "[Bobby's] mom and dad used to send me Christmas presents all the time I was growing up," she said. In the 1960s, Roberta Yano made a five-day visit to Puyallup to meet Bobby Bigelow's family. Roberta went back to Puyallup again after she was married and showed the Bigelows her wedding pictures. She and her father kept in touch with the Bigelow family over the years. "His mom was just wonderful to us," said Roberta. "I just think the world of [Bobby]." Frank Yano died in 2008.[21]

In the early 1950s, Howard Randall of Texas tried to make contact with the family of his fallen friend Eddie Myers. He even wrote to the mayor of Puyallup, who replied that the Myers family was no longer around. But Randall never forgot Eddie. In the late 1980s, Randall traveled back to the battlefields of Europe with Bill Moyers of PBS. They went to France and retraced the hard winter of 1945, and then they visited Eddie's grave amid the 262 markers belonging to the 217th Division at the American Cemetery in Luxembourg, the same cemetery where General George Patton is buried. In front of Eddie's white headstone, Randall wept as he told of the man he and many others came to love. Few other comrades have made the trip to see Eddie Myers's marker. As Randall told me in 2008, "Most of the people who knew Eddie were killed."

When Eddie's old friends from Puyallup saw the PBS special, they were stunned. Frank Hanawalt was one who saw it. "The Moyers program had quite an impact on a number of us because it showed his grave....When we saw that it was just a pivotal moment in my life."[22] For a generation of living veterans reluctant to be honored, the honor for their fallen friend was a beautiful thing.

PUYALLUP'S WAR MEMORIAL

In March 1945, a group of civic leaders representing key organizations formed a temporary committee to make plans for a Puyallup War Memorial, chaired by Rex Kelley and including Mayor Sanford Stoner, Dr. E.P. Breakey, Frank Manning, James Brown and Mrs. A.E. Ternan.[23] From this committee, an incorporation called the Puyallup Living War Memorial was formed, with its first annual meeting on May 17.[24] They agreed on a plan for a $100,000 memorial building in downtown Puyallup and began to promote the idea throughout town.

Fundraising did not go as planned. Only $20,000 was in the fund by June 1948. Chaired by builder and former mayor Steve Gray, the committee revised its plan and settled on a less expensive building. It would be a multipurpose hall in Grayland Park, a park that had been named for Gray himself, and it would be constructed of concrete blocks.[25] In this work, Gray proved to be tireless. He became an evangelist for the cause, lining up commitments of both dollars and in-kind work. Gray himself volunteered his construction expertise to make the project a reality.[26]

The committee announced a community-wide pledge campaign that summer, with help from service clubs. Ruby Grant, president of the Altrusa Club, organized a community-wide Flash Drive fundraiser with door-to-door solicitations, raising almost $25,000.[27] The Kiwanis Club was the top organizational donor in the summertime campaign, with $4,200 raised by July 29.[28]

Construction was underway in the summer of 1949, and volunteer groups rallied to help with particular tasks. Fifty Kiwanians and other volunteers spent three hours one Friday evening in August laying down about six thousand square feet of shiplap on the roof.[29] Volunteers brought their own hammers and saws to another Kiwanis work party on Tuesday, September 6, to finish off the work on the roof.[30]

Local YMCA executive and D-Day veteran Bob Leonard with an ambitious plan to expand Puyallup's War Memorial facility in the 1950s. *Puyallup Kiwanis Club Archive.*

Puyallup's War Memorial Building as it looked in 2018. *Photo by Hans Zeiger.*

The formal dedication program for the War Memorial Building was held in May 1951, with a keynote address by College of Puget Sound president R. Franklin Thompson.[31]

AN ENDURING LEGACY

Eunice Gilliam, Puyallup's phone operator during the war, made good use of the newspaper clippings she saved, her memories of the fallen friends and even bits and pieces she picked up in her job at the switchboard. It was her elementary school classmate Vernon Johnson, killed in the sinking of the USS *Liscombe Bay* in 1943, who inspired her most of all to tell the stories of Puyallup's role in the Second World War. She visited classrooms in the Puyallup schools and spoke of the heroes she had known. In 2001, Eunice lobbied the city council to erect a memorial statue to Puyallup's veterans and its fallen soldiers of World War I, World War II, the Korean War, the Vietnam War and Operation Enduring Freedom. The statue was dedicated in Pioneer Park on Memorial Day 2002. Former POW Henry Weber laid a wreath at the ceremony.[32]

The statue, sculpted by Gareth Curtiss, is the figure of a GI with rifle at side, bending down and reaching out to help a wounded comrade. The act

World War II veterans and Puyallup VFW members George Stonack and Henry Weber take part in a Memorial Day event in 1991. *Pierce County Herald* file photo, May 25, 1991. *Courtesy of Puyallup Historical Society, Pierce County Herald Collection.*

Puyallup's Veterans Memorial, sculpted by Gareth Curtiss and dedicated on Memorial Day 2002. *Photo by Hans Zeiger.*

depicted is a reminder of Puyallup's name—the generous people. Probably unbeknownst to the sculptor, it was also the closing act in the life of Bobbie Bigelow, the quiet army cavalry medic who grew up on Fruitland Avenue and aspired to be a forest ranger—he was wounded on the bridge at Manila as he treated fellow soldiers and died in an army hospital two weeks later.

Every Memorial Day and Veterans Day, hundreds of people gather in Puyallup's Pioneer Park Pavilion to honor those who served and to remember those lost in service of the country. On Memorial Day, the roll call of the men lost in service in the country's wars is read. The citizens gathered on those occasions, and all who are privileged to call Puyallup home owe a debt of gratitude to the generation of men and women who fought and won the Second World War—on the homefront, on the seas and on faraway battlefields.

NOTES

Chapter 1

1. Zeiger interview with Manford Hogman, April 15, 2008.
2. Zeiger interview with Eleanore Stemp Brecht, December 30, 2008.
3. Zeiger interview with Stanley Stemp, December 14, 2008.
4. Interview with Manford Hogman.
5. Interview with Eleanore Stemp Brecht.
6. Zeiger interview with David Brecht, December 30, 2008.
7. Program for Gertrude Wilhelmsen Memorial Service, "In Memorium," March 23, 2005; Paula Friedmann, "Puyallup Farm Girl Competed in Olympics 40 Years Ago," *Tacoma News Tribune*, 1976, clipping in Jean Glaser Collection.
8. Friedmann, "Puyallup Farm Girl Competed"; Gertrude Stelling, "'Play by Play' Account of Trip to Chicago Given by Miss Stelling," July 20, 1932 letter published in newspaper, publication date unknown, clipping in Jean Glaser Collection.
9. "Begins Today to Send Girl Athletes and Coaches to Providence for Olympic Trials," 1936, clipping in Jean Glaser Collection; Joe Nutter, "Women Track Stars Drill at Brown for Olympic Tests," 1936, clipping in Jean Glaser Collection.
10. "Sisters Leaving Today," July 3, 1936, clipping in Jean Glaser Collection.
11. Elliott Metcalf, "Puyallupites Raising Cash," *Tacoma Times*, July 10, 1936.
12. Robert O. Logan, "Sportsmanship," 1936, clipping in Gertrude Wilhelmsen scrapbook.

13. Fred L. Steers, "Track and Field Athletics—Women," *Report of the American Olympic Committee, 1936*, 151.

14. Robert O. Logan telegram to Gertrude Wilhelmsen, July 12, 1936, Gertrude Wilhelmsen scrapbook.

15. YMBC telegram to Gertrude Wilhelmsen, July 3, 1936, Jean Glaser Collection.

16. "Puyallup and the Olympics," 1936, clipping in Gertrude Wilhelmsen scrapbook.

17. Program for Gertrude Wilhelmsen Memorial Service; Lisa Pemberton-Butler, "Gertie's Once More a Part of the Olympic Tradition," *Pierce County Herald*, May 3, 1996, A5.

18. Joe Breeze, "Olympic Memories," *Pierce County Herald*, June 3, 1994, A1.

19. Lori Price and Ruth Anderson, *Puyallup: A Pioneer Paradise* (Charleston, SC: Arcadia Publishing, 2002), 98–99; Program for Gertrude Wilhelmsen Memorial Service.

20. Gertrude Wilhelmsen notes, scrapbook.

21. Daniel James Brown, *The Boys in the Boat: Nine Americans and Their Epic Quest for Gold at the 1936 Berlin Olympics* (New York: Penguin Books, 2013), 116–17.

22. Ibid., 129, 154–55, 221.

23. Ibid., 282.

24. Ibid., 285.

25. Ibid., 307.

26. Ibid., 308.

27. George Hunt letter to parents, *Puyallup Valley Tribune*, July 17, 1936, 5.

28. Letter to Mr. and Mrs. Elwood Hunt, August 5, 1936, published in the *Puyallup Valley Tribune*, August 21, 1936, 1.

29. Brown, *Boys in the Boat*, 344–47.

30. Ibid., 350–51.

31. Ibid., 154.

32. Brown, *Boys in the Boat*, 358; "When Olympic Athletes Were Honored by Valley," September 1936, clipping in Jean Glaser Collection.

33. "Puyallup's Girl Athlete Returns from Olympics," 1936, clipping in Jean Glaser Collection.

34. Stuart O. Van Slyke, *The Life of Stuart O. Van Slyke: An Autobiography, Book One, Memories of a Forgotten Age, May 1916–May 1946* (Bloomington, IN: AuthorHouse, 2006), 71.

35. Ibid., 93.

36. W.R. Sandy, meeting notes, May 23, 1940, Kiwanis Club of Puyallup Archive.

37. Ibid., August 1, 1940, Kiwanis Club of Puyallup Archive.

38. Price and Anderson, *Puyallup*, 101; *Puyallup Valley Tribune*, "Puyallup's Guard Unit to Answer Uncle Sam's Call," February 7, 1941, 1.

39. Zeiger interview with Paul Harmes, August 19, 2008.

40. Zeiger interview with Frank Hanawalt, May 7, 2008.

41. Zeiger interview with Earl White, May 12, 2008.

42. Jackson Granholm, *The Day We Bombed Switzerland: Flying with the U.S. Eighth Army Air Force in World War II* (Shrewsbury, UK: Airlife Publishing Limited, 2000), 4.

43. Royal Air Force, "The Few," https://www.raf.mod.uk/campaign/battle-of-britain-75th/the-few; John Keegan, *The Second World War* (London: Pimlico, 1997), 81.

44. *Puyallup Valley Tribune*, "Second Lieutenant Douglas Kelley, PHS '39, MIA in Pacific," 1; interview with Gloria Kelley Fredrickson, May 15, 2009.

45. Stephen L. McFarland, *Conquering the Night: Army Air Forces Night Fighters at War* (N.p.: Air Force History and Museums Program, 1997), 34–36.

46. Interview with Gloria Kelley Fredrickson, May 15, 2009; *Puyallup Valley Tribune*, "Second Lieutenant Douglas Kelley, PHS '39, MIA in Pacific," 1.

47. Major Richard Vernon Hill, *My War with Imperial Japan: Escape and Evasion* (New York: Vantage Press, 1989), 174–76.

48. Ibid., 176.

49. *The Hi-Life* 22, no. 11, "'Which Way America' Will Be Topic for Commencement Panel Discussion" (May 7, 1941): 1.

Chapter 2

1. Zeiger interview with Gene Humiston Cotton, August 19, 2008.

2. Leatrice R. Arakaki and John R. Kuborn, *7 December 1941: The Air Force Story* (Hickam Air Base, HI: Pacific Air Forces Office of History, 1991), 72–73; *Puyallup Press*, "Winner of Silver Star Citation for Gallantry to Spend Leave Here," November 27, 1942, 1.

3. *Puyallup Press*, "Many Puyallup People in Hawaii at Time of Attack by Jap Air Force," December 12, 1942, 10; *Puyallup Valley Tribune*, "Puyallup Men Fight Japanese in Pacific War," December 11, 1941, 1; Zeiger interview with Bliss Lundrigan Welcker, August 30, 2008; *Puyallup Press*, "Home on

Furlough," November 5, 1943; *Puyallup Valley Tribune*, "Son Missing on Helena," August 5, 1943, 1.

4. Zeiger interview with Ralph Smith, May 13, 2008.

5. Zeiger interview with Betty Porter Dunbar, May 14, 2008.

6. Interview with Cotton.

7. Katharine Gronen, *Christ Church: First 100 Years* (Puyallup, WA: Christ Church Episcopal, 1993), 23.

8. Zeiger interview with Marie Jones Robinson, January 13, 2008.

9. Zeiger interview with Jim Riley, May 5, 2008.

10. Ronald Magden, *Furusato: Tacoma-Pierce County Japanese, 1888–1977* (Tacoma, WA: Tacoma Longshore Book and Research Committee, 1998), 113.

11. Zeiger interview with John Watanabe, October 1, 2008.

12. Zeiger interview with Don Henderson, May 21, 2008.

13. Zeiger interview with Gilman Welcker, August 22, 2008.

14. Zeiger interview with Al Gerstmann, April 22, 2008.

15. Zeiger interview with Jane Bader Trimbley, August 7, 2008.

16. *Puyallup Valley Tribune*, "Instructions on Blackout Given by Montgomery," December 12, 1941, 1.

17. Ibid., "Large Number Hear Blackout Talks," December 12, 1941, 1.

18. Price and Anderson, *Puyallup*, 102; *Puyallup Valley Tribune*, "Instructions on Blackout Given by Montgomery," December 12, 1941, 1.

19. Price and Anderson, *Puyallup*, 102.

20. *Puyallup Valley Tribune*, "Puyallup Joins State-wide Air Raid Program," March 27, 1942, 1; "Puyallup Split into Nine Air Raid Precincts," January 2, 1942, 1.

21. W.R. Sandy, meeting notes, January 15, 1942, Kiwanis Club of Puyallup Archive; Hill, *My War with Imperial Japan*, 181–83; Price and Anderson, *Puyallup*, 102; *Puyallup Valley Tribune*, "Air Raid Post Ready to Go Men Volunteer," January 2, 1942, 1.

22. *Puyallup Valley Tribune*, "Boy Scouts to Intensify Drive for All Paper," January 23, 1942, 1.

23. Ibid., "Puyallup Will Test Defenses in Mock Raid," February 13, 1942, 1.

24. Ibid., "Observation Post in Use," August 24, 1942, 1; Price and Anderson, *Puyallup*, 102; *Puyallup Valley Tribune*, "Puyallup Post Ranks with Best in This District," November 20, 1942, 1.

25. *Puyallup Valley Tribune*, "New Dimout Regulations Will Be in Effect on August 20," August 14, 1942, 1.

26. Ibid., "Dimout Ruling Has Teeth," November 6, 1942, 1.

27. *Puyallup Press*, "Army Officials to Inspect Fair Ground Lighting," November 6, 1942, 1.

28. *Puyallup Valley Tribune*, "Dim-Out Line Was Yesterday for Civilians," November 13, 1942, 1.

29. Zeiger interview with Warren Eddy, September 18, 2008.

30. Zeiger interview with Curt Hammond, April 28, 2009.

31. Interview with Warren Eddy, September 18, 2008.

32. Andy Anderson, "Puyallup and the 260th Coastal Artillery Anti Aircraft Regiment," in e-mail to Zeiger, April 30, 2008.

33. Ibid.

34. Interview with Warren Eddy, September 18, 2008.

35. Anderson, "Puyallup and the 260th Coastal Artillery"; interview with Curt Hammond, April 28, 2009.

36. Zeiger interview with Dorothy Morris, September 16, 2008.

37. Hill, *My War with Imperial Japan*, 171–72; *Puyallup Valley Tribune*, "News Comes from Manila," January 4, 1942, 1; "Carl Gabrielson Manila Prisoner," April 3, 1942, 5.

38. Zeiger interview with Don Henderson, May 21, 2008; Zeiger interview with Jim Riley, May 5, 2008.

39. Zeiger interview with Robert Tresch, August 2, 2017; "Puyallup Youth Held Prisoner by Japanese," June 17, 1942, clipping; Susan Gordon, "Mercy!," *Port Angeles Daily News*, April 26, 1992.

40. Gordon, "Mercy!," *Port Angeles Daily News*.

41. Headquarter U.S. Army Forces in the Far East, General Order 40, Private Albert Tresch Silver Star citation, March 13, 1942.

42. Gordon, "Mercy!," *Port Angeles Daily News*.

43. *Puyallup Valley Tribune*, "Albert Tresch on Bataan Peninsula," April 10, 1942, 1.

44. Gordon, "Mercy!," *Port Angeles Daily News*.

45. *Puyallup Valley Tribune*, "Albert Tresch Missing in Action," June 12, 1942, 1; "Puyallup Youth Held Prisoner by Japanese," June 17, 1942, clipping.

Chapter 3

1. Paul Hackett interview with Eunice Barth Gilliam, March 28, 2001, South Hill Historical Society Collection.

2. *Puyallup Valley Tribune*, "Marine Recruiting Station Located at P.O.," December 26, 1941, 1.

3. *Puyallup Press*, "In Charge of Recruiting," November 20, 1942, 1.
4. *Puyallup Valley Tribune*, "Captain Griffiths Takes Enlistments," November 20, 1942, 1.
5. Ibid., "Earns Silver Star," October 30, 1942, 1.
6. Ibid., "Local Hospital Established as a Defense Base," April 3, 1942, 1.
7. Ibid., "Red Cross War Relief Fund Short," January 23, 1942, 1.
8. Ibid., "Priority Plan Announced for Valley Buses," April 3, 1942, 1.
9. Ibid., "Boy Scouts Intensify Drive for All Paper," January 23, 1942, 1.
10. Ibid., "Get in the Scrap to Fight the Japs," April 17, 1942, 1.
11. Ibid., "Individual Sugar Ration Books to Be Distributed," May 1, 1942, 1.
12. Ibid., "Tire Ration Board Issue 22 Permits," April 24, 1942, 1.
13. Ibid., "Collection of Scrap Rubber Ends July 10," July 3, 1942, 1; "Salvage Rubber Takes Spotlight," June 19, 1942, 1.
14. *Puyallup Valley Tribune*, "'Junk Rally Day' Is Sat., Aug. 29 Everyone Urged to Assist in Drive," August 28, 1942, 1.
15. Ibid., "Puyallup Meat Markets Are Bare No Relief Promised for Situation," March 25, 1943, 1.
16. Ibid., "Valleyites Give Generously in Victory Drive," May 8, 1942, 1.
17. Price and Anderson, *Puyallup*, 102.
18. *Puyallup Press*, "Puyallup Women Join Nationwide War Bond Week," November 20, 1942, 1; Price and Anderson, *Puyallup*, 102.
19. *Puyallup Valley Tribune*, "Puyallup Flier Lost in Action," July 29, 1943, 4.
20. *Puyallup Press*, "Jaycox Awarded Army Medals," December 3, 1943.
21. Ibid., "Puyallup Woman, Now a WAAC, May Win Commission," November 20, 1942, 1.
22. Ibid., "Valley Girls Complete Training," November 26, 1943.
23. Ibid., "Ward Sisters Join Army Nurse Corps," October 8, 1943.
24. *Puyallup Valley Tribune*, "Betty Gerstmann Becomes an Officer," January 7, 1943, 1.
25. Ibid., "Nurses Write from India," September 2, 1943, 1.
26. Laurie Otto letter to Norm Ward, August 3, 1943, from Dennis Ward Collection.
27. *Puyallup Valley Tribune*, "Harvest Work Plan Includes School Pupils," February 13, 1942, 1.
28. Ibid., "Soldiers Pick Berries, Eat and Have Fun," July 24, 1942, 1.
29. Ibid., "Harvesting of Raspberry Crop Looks Brighter," July 10, 1942, 1.
30. Ibid., "More Workers Aid Harvest," July 24, 1942, 1.
31. Ibid., "Puyallup Merchants Decorate Windows to Keep Daffodil Festival," April 1, 1943, 1.

32. Ibid., "Daffodil Caravan Brings Soldiers to Valley Fields," April 15, 1943, 1.

33. Ibid., "Recruiting of Boys and Girls to Assist Farmers Gets Under Way," April 8, 1943, 1.

34. Ibid., "Recruiting of Youth to Assist Farmers Is Now Under Way," June 10, 1943, 1.

35. Price and Anderson, *Puyallup*, 105.

36. *Puyallup Valley Tribune*, "People Go into Fields Over Labor Day," September 9, 1943, 1.

37. Ibid., "Puyallup Schools Will Not Open Until Sept. 21," August 14, 1942, 1.

38. Lena DiMeo, "Students, Administration Go All Out for Victory," *The Hi-Life* 25, no. 1 (October 14, 1942): 1.

39. Ibid.

40. Ibid.

41. "Sunday Is Suggested," news clipping, unknown date.

42. *The Hi Life* 25, no. 3, "War Classes Will Begin Next Month" (November 25, 1942): 1; ibid., 25, no. 4, "Organization for Victory Is Discussed" (December 23, 1942): 1.

43. *The Hi-Life* 25, no. 4, "Youth Plays Great Role, Says Langlie" (December 23, 1942): 1.

44. *The Hi-Life* 25, no. 4, "Educators Consider Problems" (December 23, 1942): 1; ibid., 25, no. 4, "Ex Teachers Hold Ranks" (December 23, 1942): 3.

45. *The Hi-Life* 25, no. 4, "Former Students Welcomed Home" (December 23, 1942): 1.

46. *Puyallup Valley Tribune*, "Christmas Mail Prospect Nears as Officials Advise V-Mail Use," November 13, 1942, 1.

47. Zeiger interview with Ken Turney, December 31, 2007.

Chapter 4

1. Zeiger interview with Frank Failor, May 14, 2008.

2. *The Hi-Life* 23, no. 4, "Chats with the Editor" (December 18, 1941): 1.

3. H.V. Starbird, "We're All Americans," *The Hi-Life* 23, no. 5 (December 18, 1941): 1.

4. Louis Fiset, *Camp Harmony: Seattle's Japanese Americans and the Puyallup Assembly Center* (Chicago: University of Illinois Press, 2009), 61.

5. Ibid., 61–63.
6. Franklin D. Roosevelt, Executive Order 9066, February 19, 1942, National Archives, https://www.archives.gov/historical-docs/todays-doc/?dod-date=219.
7. Fiset, *Camp Harmony*, 63–64.
8. Magden, *Furusato*, 163.
9. *Tacoma Times*, "Puyallup Kiwanians Vote on Removal of Japanese," February 27, 1942.
10. *Tacoma News Tribune*, "Backs Authorities in Jap Problem," February 27, 1942.
11. Fiset, *Camp Harmony*, 64.
12. Ibid., 64–66.
13. Ibid., 64–65.
14. *Puyallup Valley Tribune*, "Entire Company of Army Police to Watch Japs," April 10, 1942, 1.
15. Price and Anderson, *Puyallup*, 103; *Puyallup Valley Tribune*, "Japanese Will Be Housed Here," April 3, 1942, 1.
16. Fiset, *Camp Harmony*, 66.
17. Ibid., 71–72.
18. Ibid., 72.
19. Ibid.
20. Ibid., 77.
21. Zeiger interview with Yoshiko Yamaji Nogaki, May 14, 2009.
22. Zeiger interview with John Watanabe, October 1, 2008.
23. Zeiger interview with Bob Mizukami, April 21, 2008.
24. Interview with Mizukami.
25. Zeiger interview with Ruth Brackman Martinson, July 14, 2008.
26. Zeiger interview with Stanley Stemp, December 14, 2008.
27. Paul Hackett interview with Eunice Barth Gilliam, 2001.
28. Fiset, *Camp Harmony*, 79.
29. Zeiger interview with Frank Hanawalt, May 7, 2008.
30. Price and Anderson, *Puyallup*, 104.
31. Fiset, *Camp Harmony*, 82–84.
32. Ibid., 87.
33. Ibid., 58.
34. Ibid., 87.
35. Ibid., 97.
36. Ibid., 89.
37. Ibid., 96–97.
38. Interview with Mizukami.

39. Interview with Watanabe.

40. Fiset, *Camp Harmony*, 101–2.

41. Zeiger interview with Monica Morash Wilson, May 2008.

42. Zeiger interview with Gene Humiston Cotton, August 19, 2008.

43. Zeiger interview with Bob Ujick, December 6, 2008.

44. Fiset, *Camp Harmony*, 105.

45. Ibid., 103.

46. L.H. Tibesar, M.M. letter to the Most Reverend Gerald Shaughnessy, April 14, 1942, RG1200 Apologetics—Japanese, Relations with—Correspondence Vol. 1, 24/5, Archives of the Archdiocese of Seattle.

47. Monsignor John F. Gallagher memorandum, April 27, 1942, RG1200 Apologetics, Correspondence Vol. 1, 24/5, Archives of the Archdiocese of Seattle.

48. L.H. Tibesar, M.M. letter to the Most Reverend Gerald Shaughnessy, May 12, 1942, RG1200 Apologetics, Correspondence Vol. 1, 24/5, Archives of the Archdiocese of Seattle.

49. Letter from the Most Reverend Gerald Shaughnessy to L.H. Tibesar, M.M, May 12, 1942, from Catholic Archdiocese of Seattle Archives.

50. Fiset, *Camp Harmony*, 136–38.

51. Bill Hosokawa, *Nisei: The Quiet Americans* (New York: William Morrow and Company, 1969), 333.

52. Fiset, *Camp Harmony*, 128.

53. Ibid., 129.

54. Ibid., 132.

55. Ibid., 125.

56. *Puyallup Valley Tribune*, "Sanitary Situation Under Fire," May 15, 1942, 1.

57. Interview with Hanawalt.

58. Zeiger interview with Paul Harmes, December 29, 2007.

59. Fred Orton e-mail to Zeiger, November 28, 2017.

60. Zeiger interviews with Jeanette Whitman and Monica Morash Wilson, December 21, 2007.

61. Fiset, *Camp Harmony*, 156–57.

62. Ibid., 160–61.

63. Zeiger interview with Sue Fujikedo, August 23, 2008.

64. Fiset, *Camp Harmony*, 158–60.

65. Interview with Mizukami.

66. Fiset, *Camp Harmony*, 163.

67. Ibid., 165.

68. *Puyallup Press*, "Army Officials to Inspect Fair Ground Lighting," November 6, 1942, 1.

69. *Puyallup Valley Tribune*, "Raze Japanese Camp Buildings," September 23, 1943, 1.

70. Interview with Mizukami.

71. Zeiger interview with Mae Fujii, April 28, 2008.

72. Fiset, *Camp Harmony*, 162–63.

73. Ibid., 163.

74. Magden, *Furusato*, 151.

75. Ibid., 137.

76. Ibid., 139.

77. Interview with Fujikedo.

78. *The Hi-Life* 25, no. 3, "Old Friends Write Home" (November 4, 1942): 1.

79. Zeiger interview with Min Uchida, April 22, 2008.

80. Magden, *Furusato*, 156.

81. Interview with Mizukami.

82. Zeiger interview with Frank Mizukami, May 14, 2009.

83. Magden, *Furusato*, 161.

84. Ibid., 163.

85. Ibid.

86. Ibid., 161–62.

87. *Puyallup Valley Tribune*, "Pearl Harbor League Elects Directors," March 22, 1945, 3.

88. Ibid., "To Discuss Jap Question Tonight," January 4, 1945, 1.

89. Magden, *Furusato*, 163.

Chapter 5

1. Van Slyke, *Life of Stuart O. Van Slyke*, 216.

2. *Puyallup Valley Tribune*, "Mother Receives Letter from Chaplain," April 22, 1943, 1.

3. *Puyallup Press*, "Many Puyallup People in Hawaii at Time of Attack by Jap Air Force," Decemeber 12, 1941, 10.

4. *Puyallup Valley Tribune*, "Mother Receives Letter from Chaplain," 4; Destroyer History Foundation, "Battle of Tassafaronga," timeline, http://destroyerhistory.org/actions/index.asp?r=4280&pid=4285.

5. Andy Anderson files; Anderson e-mail to Zeiger, May 7, 2008; Anderson e-mail to Zeiger, November 7, 2017.

6. *Puyallup Press*, "Jacobs Awarded Purple Heart," September 17, 1943.

7. Ibid., "Jacobs Tells of Navy Experience," November 26, 1943.

8. Ibid., "Award Flying Cross to Staff Sgt. Blanchard," January 14, 1944.

9. Zeiger interview with Barbara Martinson Jensen, May 21, 2008.

10. *Puyallup Press*, "Two Puyallup Boys Lost in South Pacific," December 31, 1943, 1.

11. Interview with Jensen.

12. John Holm to Tynni Martinson, December 27, 1942.

13. Ibid., January 3, 1943.

14. Ibid., January 12, 1943.

15. Ibid., February 7, 1943.

16. Ibid., February 21, 1943.

17. Ibid., March 5, 1943.

18. Ibid.

19. Ibid., May 30, 1943.

20. Ibid.

21. Ibid., August 23, 1943.

22. Ibid., July 15, 1943.

23. Ibid., September 18, 1943.

24. John Holm to Martinson family, September 26, 1943.

25. Ibid.; October 3, 1943.

26. Ibid., September 26, 1943.

27. John Holm to Tynni Martinson, September 18, 1943.

28. John Holm to Martinson family, October 10, 1943.

29. Zeiger interview with Beryl Stewart, September 16, 1943.

30. Ibid.

31. John Holm to Martinson family, date unknown, 1943.

32. John Holm to Martinson children, October 29, 1943.

33. *Puyallup Press*, "Two Puyallup Boys Lost in South Pacific," December 31, 1943, 1; Zeiger interview with Bliss Lundrigan Welcker, August 30, 2008.

34. Interview with Don Henderson, May 21, 2008.

35. Interview with Jensen.

36. Rachel Smith, "For John at Tarawa," date unknown, Martinson-Carlington family collection.

37. John Holm to Tynni Martinson, August 23, 1943.

38. Zeiger interview with Del Martinson, May 16, 2008.

39. Zeiger interview with Ed Bale, October 20, 2008.

40. Zeiger interview with Doug Crotts, October 19, 2008.

41. Zeiger interview with Frank Hanawalt, May 7, 2008.

42. Ibid.; *Puyallup Press*, "Lt. Sloat Killed on Saipan," August 4, 1944, clipping from Eunice Barth Gilliam Collection.

43. *Puyallup Press*, "Lt. Sloat Killed on Saipan."

44. Eric Hammel and John E. Lane, *Bloody Tarawa: The Second Marine Division, November 20–23, 1943* (St. Paul, MN: Zenith Press, 2006), 264.

45. Tarawa on the Web, "Cobra," http://www.tarawaontheweb.org/cobra. htm.

46. Zeiger interview with Bill Eads, October 19, 2008.

47. Interview with Eads; Zeiger interview with Ed Bale, April 30, 2009.

48. Tarawa on the Web, Cobra; "Cpl. William H. Eads, Jr.," http://www. tarawaontheweb.org/billeads.htm; interview with Eads.

49. Tarawa on the Web, "Cobra."

50. Interview with Eads.

51. Tarawa on the Web, "Cpl. William H. Eads, Jr."; interview with Eads.

52. Interview with Eads.

53. Romain Cansiere and Philip Wright, "Remaining M4A2 on Betio," Tanks on Tarawa, https://www.tanksontarawa.com/m4a2-on-betio--- today.html.

54. *Puyallup Valley Tribune*, "Puyallup Meets War Loan Quota," October 7, 1943, 1; "Raze Japanese Camp Buildings," September 23, 1943, 1.

55. *Puyallup Valley Tribune*, "Mayor Praises 4-H Bond Seller," January 27, 1944, 1; "4-H Clubs Pledge to Support Bond Drive and Buy Liberty Ship," January 27, 1944, 1.

56. Interview with Bale, April 30, 2009.

57. Ibid.

58. Ibid.

59. Zeiger interview with Betty Porter Dunbar, May 14, 2008; interview with Frank Hanawalt, May 7, 2008.

60. *Puyallup Press*, "Two Local Soldiers Are Dead," August 11, 1944.

61. Zeiger interview with Roy Rinker, April 21, 2009.

62. "Ray G. Glaser Loses Life in Flaming Plane," clipping; *Puyallup Valley Tribune*, "Puyallup Airman Dies in Plane Accident," January 6, 1944, 1.

63. "Glaser Rites," clipping, date unknown.

64. Zeiger interview with Roy Rinker, April 21, 2009.

65. Zeiger interview with Jack Barker, May 21, 2009.

66. *Puyallup Press*, "Memorial Service for Dead Flyer," April 14, 1944, 1; *Puyallup Valley Tribune*, "Memorial Services for Puyallup Flyer," April 13, 1944, 1.

67. Zeiger interview with Chuck Krippahne, May 2008.

68. Interview with Hanawalt; Zeiger interview with Frank Failor, May 14, 2008.

Chapter 6

1. John Holm to Tynni Martinson, December 27, 1942.
2. Ibid., February 11, 1943.
3. George Holm to Tynni Martinson, May 16, 1943.
4. Zeiger interview with Barbara Martinson Jensen, May 21, 2008.
5. Zeiger interview with Earl White, May 12, 2008.
6. Zeiger interview with Robert Aylen, May 12, 2008.
7. Zeiger interview with Essey Kinsey Faris, May 2008.
8. "Local Flier Killed in England," clipping, date unknown; *Puyallup Valley Tribune*, "Plane Accident Takes Life of Ray Botsford," May 11, 1944, 1.
9. *Puyallup Valley Tribune*, "Sgt. Charles Watson Participates in Paratroop Invasion," July 20, 1944, 1.
10. Zeiger interview with Douglas Scott, May 19, 2008.
11. *Puyallup Press*, July 14, 1944.
12. Interview with Douglas Scott, May 19, 2008.
13. Zeiger interview with Al Gerstmann, April 22, 2008.
14. Interview with Douglas Scott, May 19, 2008.
15. Zeiger interview with Bob Leonard, April 11, 2008.
16. Interview with Gerstmann.
17. Interview with Leonard.
18. Interview with Scott.
19. Ibid.; interview with Leonard.
20. Interview with Scott.
21. Ibid.
22. Interview with Jensen.
23. *Puyallup Valley Tribune*, "Fifth War Loan Mass Meeting Shows Need of Immediate Action," June 15, 1944, 1.
24. Ibid., "Fruitland Grange Challenges Others in Bond Race," June 8, 1944, 1.
25. Price and Anderson, *Puyallup*, 102.
26. *Puyallup Press*, "General's Brother Will Speak on Flag Day," June 9, 1944; *Puyallup Valley Tribune*, "Elks to Sponsor Flag Day Parade," June 8, 1944, 1.
27. Interview with Gerstmann.
28. Zeiger interview with Dorothy Gamaunt, April 20, 2008; Zeiger interview with Dorothy Gamaunt, May 13, 2008.

Chapter 7

1. Zeiger interview with John Shirley, October 21, 2008.
2. Zeiger interview with William Ryan, March 31, 2009.
3. James R. Warren, *The War Years: A Chronicle of Washington State in World War II* (Seattle, WA: History Ink and University of Washington Press, 2000), 212.
4. Zeiger interview with David Kandle, January 12, 2008.
5. Zeiger interview with Essey Kinsey Faris, August 23, 2008.
6. Warren, *War Years*, 212.
7. Kandle letter, May 28, 1941, Kandle Family Collection.
8. The American Presidency Project, "Franklin D. Roosevelt: Radio Address Announcing an Unlimited National Emergency," http://www.presidency. ucsb.edu/ws/?pid=16120"d=16120.
9. Kandle letter, May 28, 1941, Kandle Family Collection.
10. Ibid., December 9, 1941, Kandle Family Collection.
11. Ibid., March 12, 1942, Kandle Family Collection.
12. Ibid., April 30, 1942, Kandle Family Collection.
13. Ibid., May 20, 1942; June 11, 1942, Kandle Family Collection.
14. Ibid., July 9, 1942, Kandle Family Collection.
15. Ibid., date unknown, Kandle Family Collection.
16. Ibid., August 21, 1942, Kandle Family Collection.
17. Ibid., date unknown, Kandle Family Collection.
18. Leonard Kandle letter to parents, October 10, 1942, Kandle Family Collection.
19. Kandle letter, May 19, 1943, Kandle Family Collection.
20. Ibid., January 4, 1942, Kandle Family Collection.
21. Ibid., January 7, 1942, Kandle Family Collection.
22. Ibid., January 12, 1943, Kandle Family Collection.
23. Ibid., January 14, 1943, Kandle Family Collection.
24. Ibid., February 27, 1943, Kandle Family Collection.
25. Ibid., March 9, 1943, Kandle Family Collection.
26. Ibid.
27. Ibid., March 26, 1943, Kandle Family Collection.
28. Ibid., April 21, 1943, Kandle Family Collection.
29. Ibid., April 23, 1943, Kandle Family Collection.
30. Ibid.
31. Ibid.
32. Ibid., May 29, 1943, Kandle Family Collection.
33. Ibid.
34. Ibid., June 10, 1943, Kandle Family Collection.

35. Ibid., July 23, 1943, Kandle Family Collection.

36. Ibid.

37. Ibid., July 1943, Kandle Family Collection.

38. Ibid., August 12, 1943, Kandle Family Collection.

39. Ibid., August 16, 1943, Kandle Family Collection.

40. Ibid., August 28, 1943, Kandle Family Collection.

41. Ibid.

42. Ibid., September 1943, Kandle Family Collection.

43. Ibid., September 20, 1943, Kandle Family Collection.

44. Ibid., October 5, 1943, Kandle Family Collection.

45. Ibid., October 12, 1943, Kandle Family Collection.

46. Ibid.

47. Ibid., November 5, 1943; and November 16, 1943, Kandle Family Collection.

48. Ibid., November 5, 1943, Kandle Family Collection.

49. Ibid., November 29, 1943, Kandle Family Collection.

50. Ibid., December 30, 1943, Kandle Family Collection.

51. Ibid., February 7, 1944, Kandle Family Collection.

52. Ibid., February 20, 1944, Kandle Family Collection.

53. Ibid., March 7, 1944, Kandle Family Collection.

54. Ibid., April 9, 1944, Kandle Family Collection.

55. Mark Porter, "Private Mark Porter Describes Preparations for Anzio Attack," *Puyallup Valley Tribune*, March 10, 1944.

56. Zeiger interview with Manuel Moreno, March 19, 2009.

57. Kandle letter, May 1, 1944, Kandle Family Collection.

58. Ibid.

59. Zeiger interview with Maurice Kendall, March 12, 2009.

60. Kandle letter, May 10, 1944, Kandle Family Collection.

61. Ibid., May 11, 1944, Kandle Family Collection.

62. Ibid., May 13, 1944, Kandle Family Collection.

63. Ibid., May 24, 1944, Kandle Family Collection.

64. Ibid., May 1944., Kandle Family Collection.

65. Ibid.

66. Ibid., July 31, 1944, Kandle Family Collection.

67. Mark Porter letter to M.F. Porter and Alma Porter, June 26, 1944, published in *Puyallup Valley Tribune*, "Mark Porter Writes Graphic Descriptions of His Visits to Rome," July 20, 1944, 1.

68. Kandle letter, June 26, 1944, Kandle Family Collection.

69. Ibid., July 13, 1944, Kandle Family Collection.

70. Ibid., July 19, 1944, Kandle Family Collection.

71. Ibid., July 28, 1944, Kandle Family Collection.
72. Ibid., July 31, 1944, Kandle Family Collection.
73. Ibid., 1944, Kandle Family Collection.
74. Ibid., September 1, 1944, Kandle Family Collection.
75. Ibid., September 10, 1944, Kandle Family Collection.
76. Ibid., September 14, 1944, Kandle Family Collection.
77. Ibid., September 18, 1944, Kandle Family Collection.
78. Ibid., September 23, 1944, Kandle Family Collection.
79. Ibid., October 12, 1944, Kandle Family Collection.
80. Ibid.
81. Ibid.
82. Ibid., date unknown, 1944, Kandle Family Collection.
83. Ibid., 1944, Kandle Family Collection.
84. Ibid.
85. Ibid., October 20, 1944, Kandle Family Collection.
86. Ibid.
87. Ibid., November 11, 1944, Kandle Family Collection.
88. Kandle letter to parents, November 13, 1944, Kandle Family Collection.
89. Ibid.
90. Kandle letter to grandparents, November 13, 1944, Kandle Family Collection.
91. Kandle letter to parents, November 13, 1944, Kandle Family Collection.
92. Zeiger interview with William Ryan, March 12, 2009
93. Kandle letter, December 7, 1944, Kandle Family Collection.
94. Ibid., December 15, 1944, Kandle Family Collection.
95. Ibid., December 19, 1944, Kandle Family Collection.
96. John Shirley, *I Remember: Stories of a Combat Infantryman in World War II* (Livermore, CA: self-published, 2009), 64–66.
97. Ibid., 67–68.
98. Eugene Jacobsen letter to John Shirley, date unknown.
99. Zeiger interview with George Dittoe, March 19, 2009.
100. Eugene Jacobsen letter to John Shirley.
101. Ibid.
102. Interview with William Ryan.
103. Eugene Jacobsen letter to John Shirley.
104. Zeiger interview with Whitney Mullen, March 25, 2009.
105. Eugene Jacobsen letter to John Shirley; interview with William Ryan.
106. Van Slyke, *Life of Stuart O. Van Slyke*, 304.
107. Marigene Kandle letter to Mr. and Mrs. C.C. Kandle, March 7, 1945, reference to Major General J.A. Ulio letter to Marigene Kandle.

108. Cliff and Eloise letter to Mr. and Mrs. C.C. Kandle, March 9, 1945.

109. Chaplain letter to Marigene Kandle, February 23, 1945.

110. Ibid.

111. Marigene Kandle letter to Mr. and Mrs. C.C. Kandle, March 7, 1945.

112. Zeiger interview with Frank Hanawalt, May 7, 2008.

113. Shirley, *I Remember*, 72–73.

114. Interview with Mullen.

115. Warren, *War Years*, 213.

116. Interview with Mullen.

Chapter 8

1. Zeiger interview with Stanley Stemp, December 14, 2008; Zeiger interview with Eleanore Stemp Brecht, December 30, 2008; *Puyallup Valley Tribune*, "Wounded in Action," February 22, 1944, 1.

2. Ibid., "Gordon Barker Killed in Action," February 8, 1945, 1.

3. Ibid., "Three Puyallup Men Killed in Action," March 1945, 1.

4. Interview with Stanley Barker, August 4, 2017.

5. *Puyallup Valley Tribune*, "Wounded in Action," February 22, 1944, 1.

6. Interview with Brecht.

7. Virgil Harwood, *Hi-Life Hi-Lite*, no. 30 (October 2006): 3.

8. Interview with Brecht.

9. Harwood, *Hi-Life Hi-Lite*.

10. Interview with Brecht.

11. Interview with Stemp.

12. *Puyallup Valley Tribune*, "Hold Memorial for Elmer L. Stemp," March 1945, 1.

13. John Hill, "Puyallup WWII Vet Gets Letter from Befriended Polish Youth," *News Tribune*, July 1990.

14. Interview with Stemp.

15. Hill, "Puyallup WWII Vet Gets Letter from Befriended Polish Youth."

16. Interview with Faris.

17. Zeiger interview with Frank Hanawalt, May 7, 2008.

18. Ibid.

19. Interview with Don Henderson, May 21, 2008.

20. Interview with Aylen.

21. Zeiger interview with Manford Hogman, April 15, 2008.

22. Interview with Manford Hogman.

23. Interview with Faris.

24. Randall letter to Zeiger, September 20, 2008.

25. Ibid.

26. Zeiger interview with Howard Randall, January 12, 2008.

27. Ibid.

28. U.S. Army, History of the 76th Infantry Division, http://www.history.army.mil/documents/eto-ob/76ID-ETO.htm, 46–47.

29. Interview with Randall.

30. Howard M. Randall, *War Chronicle: An Infantryman with Patton* (Austin, TX: Sunbelt Media, 2001), 24–35.

31. Randall letter to Zeiger, September 20, 2008.

32. Randall, *War Chronicle*, 24–35.

33. Ibid., 46.

34. Ibid., 55.

35. Ibid., 54; interview with Randall.

36. Eddie Myers letter, Puyallup Historical Society Collection.

37. Randall, *War Chronicle*, 54.

38. Ibid., 54–55.

39. Ibid., 76.

40. Ibid.

41. Ibid., 77.

42. Ibid., 78.

43. Ibid., 86.

44. PBS NOW, "NOW Transcript," June 4, 2004, http://www.pbs.org/now/transcript/transcript323_full.html.

45. See Jackson Granholm, *The Day We Bombed Switzerland: Flying with the U.S. Eighth Army Air Force in World War II* (Shrewsbury, UK: Airlife Publishing Limited, 2000), 8.

46. Ibid., 1–30.

47. Ibid., 58.

48. Ibid., 50.

49. Ibid., 64.

50. Ibid., 67, 72.

51. Ibid., 120.

52. Ibid., 141.

53. Ibid., 162.

54. Ibid., 173.

55. Ibid., 227.

56. Zeiger interview with Betty Porter Dunbar, May 15, 2008; *Puyallup Valley Tribune*, "Pfc. Mark Porter Killed in Action," May 3, 1945, 1.

57. Interview with Dunbar.

58. Mark Porter letter to M.F. and Alma Porter, April 17, 1944.

59. Ibid.

60. Ibid., August 17, 1944.

61. Ibid., November 13, 1944.

62. Ibid., October 31, 1944.

63. Bronze Star citation, December 8, 1944, Private First Class Mark F. Porter, infantry, Company K, 15th Infantry Regiment; see Colonel Eugene Tarr letter to Alma Porter, April 22, 1959, Betty Porter Dunbar Collection.

64. Shirley, *I Remember*, 72–73; interview with Dunbar.

65. *Puyallup Valley Tribune*, "Pfc. Mark Porter Killed in Action," clipping from Betty Porter Dunbar Collection.

66. Zeiger interview with Frank Failor, May 14, 2008.

67. Memorial service program, Mark Porter memorial service, Betty Porter Dunbar Collection.

68. Interview with Dunbar.

69. Zeiger interview with Dorothy Gamaunt, May 13, 2008.

70. *Puyallup Valley Tribune*, "News of Son from Anzio Beach Head," April 20, 1944, 5.

71. Interview with Gamaunt.

72. Zeiger interview with Barbara Martinson Jensen, May 21, 2008.

73. Zeiger interview with Douglas Scott, May 19, 2008.

74. *Puyallup Valley Tribune*, "Puyallup Kiwanis Club Backs United National Clothing Drive," April 6, 1945.

75. Zeiger interview with Cliff Merriott, May 29, 2009.

76. Ibid.

77. *Puyallup Valley Tribune*, "Puyallup Churches Plan V-E Services," May 3, 1945, 1.

Chapter 9

1. Zeiger interview with Bill Hogman, April 21, 2008.

2. Carl Vest, "Balloon Bombs of 1945 Rocked South Hill," *Puyallup Herald*, April 8, 2015, http://www.thenewstribune.com/news/local/community/puyallup-herald/ph-opinion/article26276437.html; Carl Vest and South Hill Historical Society, "History: Recalling the Unique Bombing of South Hill in 1945," *Puyallup Herald*, March 10 2016, http://www.thenewstribune.com/news/local/community/puyallup-herald/ph-

opinion/article65219512.html; Carl Vest, "South Hill Bombed during World War II," South Hill Historical Society, http://southhillhistory.com/History/Balloon_Bombs.html.

3. Zeiger interview with Ruth Bigelow Jones, May 2008.

4. Zeiger interview with Roberta Yano Johnson, September 15, 2008.

5. *Puyallup Press*, "News About Service Men," April 28, 1944, 1.

6. *Puyallup Valley Tribune*, "News Notes of Servicemen," September 16, 1943, 1.

7. Robert Bigelow letter to Vina Bigelow, November 6, 1944.

8. Robert Bigelow letter in Ruth Bigelow Jones Collection.

9. Robert Bigelow letter to Vina Bigelow, December 4, 1944.

10. *Puyallup Valley Tribune*, "Letter Tells of Act of Heroism," April 12, 1945, 1.

11. Ibid., "Writes From Manila Rest Camp," March 1945, 1.

12. Ibid., "Release Local Man from Prison Camp," March 1945, 1.

13. Letter from Carl Gabrielson to his wife, published in *Puyallup Valley Tribune*, April 19, 1945, 4.

14. *Tacoma Times*, "Americans in Jap Prison Camps Ate Cats and Dogs to Keep Alive," June 29, 1945.

15 *Tacoma News Tribune*, "Into Marines," September 8, 1943.

16. *Puyallup Valley Tribune*, "Viking Pilot," March 4, 1943, 1.

17. Harold Shaw, "Calling the Shots," *Puyallup Valley Tribune*, February 25, 1943, 7.

18. Zeiger interview with Bob Ujick, December 6, 2008.

19. Ibid.

20. *Puyallup Valley Tribune*, "Dick Porenta Killed On Okinawa Island," May 24, 1945.

21. Zeiger interview with Bob Ujick, December 6, 2008.

22. Zeiger interview with Warren Drotz, May 26, 2008.

23. Interview with Henderson.

24. Zeiger interview with Rich Holthusen, August 16, 2008.

Chapter 10

1. Hill, *My War with Imperial Japan*, 184–85.

2. Ibid., 185–88.

3. Ibid., 234.

4. Ibid., 237, 253.

5. Ibid., 237.

6. Ibid., 238–39.

7. Ibid., 240.

8. Ibid., 253–54.

9. Ibid., 257–59.

10. Ibid., 263.

11. Ibid., 265.

12. Ibid., 266–68.

13. Ibid., 271.

14. Ibid., 272.

15. Ibid., 273.

16. Ibid., 274–80.

17. Ibid., 282–83.

18. Ibid., 284.

19. Ibid., 285.

20. Ibid., 292–93.

21. Ibid., 293.

22. Ibid., 293–95.

23. Ibid., 295–96.

24. Hill, letter to VFW Post, March 26, 1945.

25. Hill, *My War with Imperial Japan*, 296.

26. Ibid., 297.

27. Ibid., 301.

28. Ibid., 306.

29. Ibid., 307.

30. *Washington Post*, "Louise Ann Lyon," October 30, 2011, via Legacy. com, http://www.legacy.com/obituaries/washingtonpost/obituary.aspx ?page=lifestory&pid=154312930#fbLoggedOut; J. Arthur Bloom, "The Spy Next Door," *American Conservative*, January 11, 2013, http://www. theamericanconservative.com/2013/01/11/the-spy-next-door.

31. Larry Bargmeyer, note to Zeiger, February 25, 2018.

32. Ibid.; Bloom, "Spy Next Door."

33. Hill, *My War with Imperial Japan*, 334.

34. Ibid., 337.

35. Ibid., 339–40.

36. Ibid., 340.

37. Ibid., 341–42.

38. Ibid., 344.

39. Ibid., 346–47.

40. Ibid., 348.
41. Ibid.
42. Ibid.
43. Ibid., 355.
44. Ibid., 356.
45. Ibid.
46. Ibid., 360.
47. Ibid., 372–73.

Chapter 11

1. *Puyallup Press*, "Tresches Hear Again from Son," September 17, 1943, 1.
2. *Puyallup Valley Tribune*, "Mrs. Robert Tresch Wins Slogan Contest," October 14, 1943, 1.
3. Ibid.; "Names of Men Killed in Service Placed on Plaque," June 15, 1944, 1.
4. Center for Research: Allied POWs in Japan, "Prisoner of War Camp #1, Fukuoka, Japan," http://mansell.com/pow_resources/camplists/fukuoka/fuk_01_fukuoka/fukuoka_01/Page01.htm#Locations.
5. Frank N. Lovato and Francisco L. Lovato, *Survivor: An American Soldier's Heartfelt Story of Intense Fighting, Surrender, and Survival from Bataan to Nagasaki* (Nevada City, CA: Del Oro Press, 2008), 205.
6. Ibid., 204–7.
7. Gordon, "Mercy!," *Port Angeles Daily News*.
8. Lovato and Lovato, *Survivor*, 207.
9. Ibid., 208.
10. Ibid., 219.
11. Ibid., 220.
12. Ibid., 221.
13. Ibid., 224–25.
14. Ibid., 227.
15. Ibid., 230–31.
16. Ibid., 232–33.
17. Ibid., 233.
18. Ibid.
19. Gordon, "Mercy!," *Port Angeles Daily News*.
20. Lovato and Lovato, *Survivor*, 234–35.
21. Ibid., 235.

22. Ibid., 236.

23. Ibid., 242–48.

24. Ibid., 248.

25. Ibid., 249.

26. Zeiger interview with Del Martinson, May 16, 2008.

27. Zeiger interview with James Tresch, May 2008.

Chapter 12

1. Van Slyke, *Life of Stuart O. Van Slyke*, 315, 319.

2. Ibid., 320.

3. Ibid., 324.

4. Ibid., 324–25.

5. Ibid., 325.

6. Ibid., 325–26.

7. Ibid., 326.

8. Ibid.

9. *Puyallup Valley Tribune*, "Dick Graves Now Believed Killed," October 18, 1945.

10. Ibid., "Sgt. Johnson Lost at Sea in Plane," April 4, 1946.

11. Zeiger interview with Eleanore Stemp Brecht, December 30, 2008.

12. Zeiger interview with Yoshiko Yamaji Nogaki, May 14, 2009.

13. Magden, *Furusato*, 171–74.

14. Zeiger interview with Bob Mizukami, April 21, 2008.

15. Hill, *My War with Imperial Japan*, v.

16. Zeiger interview with Whitney Mullen, July 21, 2009.

17. Zeiger interview with Robert Aylen, May 2008.

18. Interview with Brecht; Obituary, Stanley Stemp records.

19. Zeiger interview with Bill Hogman, April 21, 2008; Zeiger interview with Manford Hogman, April 15, 2008.

20. Interview with Bill Hogman.

21. Zeiger interview with Roberta Johnson, September 15, 2008.

22. PBS NOW, "NOW Transcript," June 4, 2004, http://www.pbs.org/now/transcript/transcript323_full.html; Zeiger interview with Howard Randall, January 12, 2008; Zeiger interview with Frank Hanawalt, May 7, 2008.

23. *Puyallup Valley Tribune*, "Lay Plans for War Memorial Committee," March 1945.

24. Ibid., "War Memorial Elect Directors," May 24, 1945.

25. Price and Anderson, *Puyallup*, 107.

26. W.R. Sandy, meeting notes, November 4, 1948.

27. *Puyallup Valley Tribune*, "Ruby Grant Given Award By Kiwanians," January 13, 1949.

28. W.R. Sandy, meeting notes, July 15, 1948, July 22, 1948, July 29, 1948; Kiwanis Club Bulletin, July 29, 1948.

29. W.R. Sandy, meeting notes, August 25, 1949; Kiwanis Club Bulletin, September 1, 1949.

30. Kiwanis Club Bulletin, September 8, 1949.

31. Price and Anderson, *Puyallup*, 107.

32. Paul Hackett interview with Eunice Barth Gilliam, 2001; Anna King, "Reaching Out to Honor Veterans," *Puyallup Herald*, May 24, 2001, 1B; Rebecca Wells, "Grateful Community Gives Thanks," *Puyallup Herald*, May 30, 2002, A1, A3.

INDEX

ABOUT THE AUTHOR

 ans Zeiger is an author, Washington state senator and local historian. He began writing about the World War II generation in Puyallup, Washington, as a columnist for the *Puyallup Herald* in 2008 and 2009. His writings have also appeared in the *Seattle Times*, the *Philadelphia Inquirer*, *American Legion* magazine, *Columbia* magazine and *HistoryLink*, and he was previously a contributing writer for *Philanthropy Daily.*

A state legislator since 2011, Hans is a trustee of the Washington State Historical Society and a member of the Washington State Legislative Oral History Advisory Board. He serves in the Washington Air National Guard. He is an active member of the Puyallup Historical Society and the South Hill Historical Society.

The son, grandson and great-grandson of Puyallup teachers, Hans is a 2003 Puyallup High School graduate. He holds a BA in American studies from Hillsdale College and a master's degree in public policy from Pepperdine University.